AMERICANS AND THE BIRTH OF ISRAEL

AMERICANS AND THE BIRTH OF ISRAEL

Lawrence J. Epstein

South Huntington Public Library
145 Pidgeon Hill Road
Huntington Station, NY 11746

ROWMAN & LITTLEFIELD
Lanham • Boulder • New York • London

Published by Rowman & Littlefield
A wholly owned subsidiary of
The Rowman & Littlefield Publishing Group, Inc.
4501 Forbes Boulevard, Suite 200, Lanham, Maryland 20706
https://rowman.com

Unit A, Whitacre Mews, 26-34 Stannary Street, London SE11 4AB, United Kingdom

Copyright © 2017 by Rowman & Littlefield

All rights reserved. No part of this book may be reproduced in any form or by any electronic or mechanical means, including information storage and retrieval systems, without written permission from the publisher, except by a reviewer who may quote passages in a review.

British Library Cataloguing in Publication Information Available

Library of Congress Cataloging-in-Publication Data

Names: Epstein, Lawrence J. (Lawrence Jeffrey), author.
Title: Americans and the birth of Israel / Lawrence J. Epstein.
Description: Lanham, Maryland : Rowman & Littlefield, [2017] | Includes bibliographical references and index.
Identifiers: LCCN 2016058253 (print) | LCCN 2016058741 (ebook) | ISBN 9781442271227 (cloth : alk. paper) | ISBN 9781442271234 (electronic)
Subjects: LCSH: Palestine—History—Partition, 1947. | Israel—History—Declaration of Independence, 1948. | Israel—Foreign relations—United States. | United States—Foreign relations—Israel.
Classification: LCC DS126.4 .E65 2017 (print) | LCC DS126.4 (ebook) | DDC 956.94/04—dc23
LC record available at https://lccn.loc.gov/2016058253

∞ ™ The paper used in this publication meets the minimum requirements of American National Standard for Information Sciences Permanence of Paper for Printed Library Materials, ANSI/NISO Z39.48-1992.

Printed in the United States of America

South Huntington Public Library

145 Pidgeon Hill Road
Huntington Station, NY 11746
(631) 549-4411
www.shpl.info

DATE DUE SLIP

Item(s) listed below were checked out to:
21974008030018

on 09/08/2017

TITLE: The prisoner in his palace :
BARCODE: 30652005096286
DUE DATE: 09-29-17 00:00AM

TITLE: Americans and the birth of Israel /
BARCODE: 30652005101094
DUE DATE: 09-29-17 00:00AM

This book is dedicated to my grandchildren:
LILY, GRAYSON, EMILIA, THEA, and ESTELLE
They bring to me the greatest gifts of all: love, hope, and unending tomorrows.

CONTENTS

Acknowledgments	ix
Major Characters	xv
Introduction	1
1 The Secret Meeting	11
2 The United Nations and the White House: The Vote for Partition	25
3 Organizing for Action	55
4 Planes and Ships and Weapons	89
5 The Irgun's Way	115
6 From Survivors to Immigrants	131
Conclusion: The Lessons for America and Israel	163
Chronology	167
References	171
Index	175

ACKNOWLEDGMENTS

It is overwhelming, exciting, inspiring, and humbling to research and write a book about so significant and historic an event as the birth of Israel and how Americans contributed to that birth. As I worked on the book, I thought of Rabbi Tarfon's famous words in the Talmud: "You are not expected to complete the task, but neither are you free to abandon it." Writing about the birth pains of a nation reborn after its people spent two thousand years in exile involved doing research that was beyond my abilities, for in principle that research should include mastering material that is both staggering in scope and in a wide variety of foreign languages. On the other hand, I had my enthusiasm and a sense of relief that so much of the material is at least available. Happily, the founders of Israel were not shy about dipping their pens in ink and attaching their thoughts to paper. They had much to say to each other and to the world. However, what I write about involves work primarily done in secret, deliberately away from prying eyes.

I first heard part of the story in this book after I read Leonard Slater's groundbreaking work of journalism, *The Pledge*. The reason for that book's importance is that Slater told the story of Americans helping arm the Palestinian Jews for the first time and conducted numerous interviews. While I have included individuals he didn't discuss and research that was then unknown or restricted, I want to start out by noting that this book, as well as any other about Americans gathering weapons and money for Israel, can't be undertaken without standing on Slater's shoulders.

I have, given the voluminous amount of material, therefore written this book not with the idea that every last fact about the subject is present. Rather, it is my goal to tell the story of Americans who aided the birth of Israel in a clear and coherent way in order to introduce readers to a vital and significant subject about perhaps the most positive event in modern Jewish history. I only hope I have successfully conveyed the depth of my own fascination with the subject.

Beyond the materials mentioned in the references section at the end of the book, I have relied on the help of a variety of very kind people. Because many of the principals in this story are deceased, I made use of a wide variety of Jewish archives. The archivists provided suggestions and very quick and useful support. Archivists and librarians are indispensable to works of this kind.

In particular, I'd like to thank:

American Jewish Archives. I would like to thank Kevin Proffitt, whose bibliographical advice and help I have sought and received for many books; Joe Weber; and the entire archives staff.

American Jewish Historical Society. For their knowledge and help, I would particularly like to thank Susan L. Malbin, director of library and archives; Boni Joi Koelliker, photo/reference archivist; Tanya Elder, senior archivist; Judi Garner, director of the American Jewish Historical Society–New England Archives (AJHS-NEA); and Stephanie Call, the collections management archivist at AJHS-NEA.

The American Jewish Joint Distribution Committee Archives.

Irit Amiel, a Holocaust survivor who made the dangerous journey to the Land of Israel on the "illegal" ship the *Hatikvah*, on which the heroic American volunteer Murray S. Greenfield also sailed. Irit, author of *Scorched: A Collection of Short Stories on Survivors (Library of Holocaust Testimonies)*, was kind enough to contact me. Murray Greenfield wrote the definitive book on American volunteers who saved Holocaust

ACKNOWLEDGMENTS

refugees and brought them to their ancient homeland in his book *The Jews' Secret Fleet*.

Arnold Berger, PhD, the editor and webkeeper at www.ClevelandJewishHistory.net, who is an expert on the extraordinarily influential Rabbi Abba Hillel Silver. I thank Dr. Berger for his guidance about Rabbi Silver.

Charlotte Bonelli, the director of the American Jewish Committee's Archives and Records Center.

Ami Eden, CEO and executive editor, 70 Faces Media, and Danielle Okrent, chief of staff, 70 Faces Media, for their guidance regarding the Jewish Telegraphic Agency Archive. www.jta.org/jta-archive/archive-page.

Dr. Rafael Medoff, director, the David S. Wyman Institute for Holocaust Studies, and author of *Militant Zionism in America*.

The National Archives, British Foreign Office.

The Truman Library. The material I read that was particularly useful included the Eddie Jacobson correspondence on Israel, the Chaim Weizmann Oral Interviews, and correspondence on Israel (from the Weizmann Institute).

Other significant help came from friends. Dr. Richard Tuckman provided ongoing articles as well as frequent and very useful conversations about Israel. Sue Rubinstein DeMasi has been a friend who, luckily for me, is also an excellent librarian, researcher, and writer. I thank her for her constant support. I highly recommend her book on Henry Alsberg, the director of the Federal Writers' Project. David Lehman and Stacey Harwood of *The Best American Poetry Blog* (http://blog.bestamericanpoetry.com/) could be the accompanying illustrations to the definitions of *kind* and *supportive*. David, a world-famous poet and editor, was generous enough to ask me to contribute to the blog, and I have frequently used that opportunity to clarify my ideas about Israel. Tony DiFranco and I meet regularly for lunch to discuss our writing. Tony's own writing and filmmaking career make him an inspiring and insightful person with whom to discuss my work. Doug Rathgeb has been a close friend for over fifty years. We've been carrying on a conversation about our writing careers for all those decades, and we continue to do so. My Facebook friends, Twitter followers, and others on the various social media platforms in which I participate support and on occasion challenge me. I appreciate all of them very much.

I'd also like to thank my spiritual leaders over the years, including my current one, Rabbi Sharon Sobel. Some of the previous people I've turned to for spiritual and other advice include, in reverse chronological order, Rabbi Stephen Karol, Rabbi Adam Fisher, Rabbi Howard Hoffman, and Rabbi Moshe Edelman. The late Rabbi Arthur Gilbert was a great influence on me when I was quite young.

I've been writing about Israel for many decades, and as a result some of the material I've previously gathered proved particularly helpful for this book. The late Amos Elon, author of a remarkable biography of Theodor Herzl, was kind enough to talk to me about his work. The late Alfred Kazin, one of America's premier literary critics, wrote a revealing letter to me about Herzl's quest for leadership. The late Reverend Isaac C. Rottenberg, then executive director of the National Christian Leadership Conference for Israel, patiently answered many questions and provided much material about Christian Zionism. I'd also like to thank the then director of the old Herzl Museum, which I visited several decades ago. By good luck, I got to be the guide there as I gave my tour group an overview of Herzl's life.

I learned an enormous amount about Israel not only from trips there but also by serving as an adviser on Israel for Congressman William Carney and Congressman Michael Forbes. Bill and Mike were extraordinarily generous in providing me with such an opportunity.

I also learned a great deal from working with former congressman Steve Israel, who was then working with the American Jewish Congress.

My great friend Assemblyman Michael Fitzpatrick, whom I met while working in Bill Carney's office, has listened to me give lectures about Israel with the patience and support that only a true friend can provide. He and his family are really an extended part of my own.

ACKNOWLEDGMENTS

All authors, understandably, thank their editors. In my case, Sarah Stanton deserves more than thanks. Her patience, support, and insights are invaluable. This is the third book we've worked on together, and I really appreciate Sarah's wisdom in guiding a book through its sometimes-rocky career from idea to publication. All the people at Rowman & Littlefield work very hard to produce good material, and I deeply appreciate their efforts.

While I have greatly profited from all this help, I bear sole responsibility for the book's contents. Surely, those who helped me have some interpretations of the material that differ from mine. Their help is not tantamount to agreement with what I have written. I am the one who assembled the facts and interpretations in this book.

My family is an indispensable part of my life that I most cherish. My brother, Richard, is my first reader. We have conversations virtually daily about Israel and much else. His wife, Perla; children, Adam and Sondra; and their families are always supportive. My cousins Toby Everett and her brother Dr. Sheldon Scheinert have discussed Israel with me for many decades. It is hard to say how very much, from childhood on, their being there has meant. My cousin Dr. Joseph Gastwirth has been so supportive that he has actually shown up for lectures I have given. His brother, my late cousin Don Gastwirth, was a literary adviser to me for many years. I miss his immense wit and knowledge.

My wife, Sharon, is there all the time when I need support. In fact, it was Sharon who many, many years ago suggested I buy a book on the history of Zionism when I wasn't sure we could afford it. It was that book that ignited what would emerge as a lifelong interest. Our children, their spouses, and their children provide both of us with unending joy. My son, Dr. Michael Epstein, is a filmmaker and musician. His wife, Sophia Cacciola, is always there to be part of his artistic world. My oldest daughter, Dr. Elana Reiser, is a mathematics professor and author. Her husband, Justin, and I have frequent conversations about books. Their daughter, Lily, is beautiful, charming, and funny. I see her every week. So far, we've read a lot of good books and celebrated Jewish holidays together. Lily keeps telling me of her plans to go to

Israel, so I have hopes that one day she and I will have discussions about her travels. My daughter Rachel Eddey, a deputy director at Columbia University, has the "joy" of listening to me constantly ask her questions about writing. That's how much I trust her judgment. Her husband, John, and I converse about politics and much else. I call on John when I deal with an uncooperative computer and need someone to fix the technical problems. Their children, Grayson and Thea, are so beautiful and talented. Grayson was in his first movie when he was two weeks old. He played a baby having a bris. Since he had personally rehearsed for the part, he did wonderfully. Lisa Christen is my youngest daughter. She's worked at the Department of Defense and is now living in Switzerland, working on projects to help women. Lisa developed my website, www.lawrencejepstein.com. Lisa's husband, Florian, is an extraordinary, helpful, and supportive husband and father. Their children, Emilia and Estelle, are so adorable and sweet.

I have dedicated this book to my grandchildren not only because I love them but also because for me they nurture a belief in the future. If, as the saying goes, grandchildren are the consolation for aging, I feel very deeply consoled.

These are the people who have made it possible for me to write this book. I thank them wholeheartedly.

MAJOR CHARACTERS

Alper, Phil. A young engineer who assisted Haim Slavin in acquiring machinery.
Arazi, Yehuda. A Haganah agent assigned to the United States to get weapons.
Aronowitz, Ike. The captain of the ship *Exodus*.
Ash, Bill. A former captain in the merchant marine who helped acquire ships.
Austin, Warren. American ambassador to the United Nations.
Ben-Gurion, David. The leader of the Jewish community in the Land of Israel.
Clifford, Clark. President Harry S. Truman's legal adviser and counselor.
Cohen, Mickey. A Jewish gangster who wanted to help Jews who defended themselves.
Crum, Bartley. An American attorney who supported the emerging Jewish state.
Dostrovsky, Jacob (later Yaakov Dori). The first head of the Haganah delegation in the United States and the overall coordinator of all efforts to get money and materials from the United States to the Land of Israel.
Greenspun, Hank. A major supplier of machine guns and airplane parts.

Hecht, Ben. A screenwriter, novelist, playwright, and activist. He wrote the pro-Zionist play *A Flag Is Born*.

Hoover, J. Edgar. Director of the Federal Bureau of Investigation.

Jacobson, Eddie. A former business partner and friend of President Truman.

Kollek, Teddy. Replaced Shlomo Rabinowitz as Haganah leader.

Marcus, Col. Mickey. An American soldier who volunteered to train the Jews in the Land of Israel.

Marshall, George C. President Truman's secretary of state.

Meyerson (later Meir), Golda. A Jewish leader in the Land of Israel who was sent to raise funds.

Montor, Henry. Director of the United Jewish Appeal.

Niles, David K. A trusted aide to President Truman who turned out to be crucial in getting support for the United Nations' partition vote.

Rabinowitz (later Shamir), Shlomo. Replaced Jacob Dostrovsky as Haganah leader.

Schwimmer, Al. Smuggled war surplus planes and recruited pilots for the Israeli Air Force.

Silver, Rabbi Abba Hillel. A Zionist activist in the United States.

Slavin, Haim. In charge of acquiring needed machinery and weapons.

Sonneborn, Rudolf. A Jewish businessman and indispensable organizer of the Sonneborn Institute.

Truman, Harry S. The president of the United States.

Weizmann, Chaim. A Zionist leader and one whom Truman learned to trust and admire.

Wise, Rabbi Stephen. An American Zionist activist.

INTRODUCTION

Frank Sinatra. Marlon Brando. Groucho Marx. Harpo Marx. Eleanor Roosevelt. Bob Hope. Milton Berle. Leonard Bernstein. Carl Reiner. The great singer and actor Paul Robeson. Actors and entertainers such as Jimmy Durante. Vincent Price, Sir Cedric Hardwicke, Burgess Meredith, Stella Adler, and Paul Muni. The boxing legend and war hero Barney Ross. Hubert Humphrey, then a mayor and eventually vice president of the United States. Dr. Ruth. Pee-wee Herman's father. And then there were the mobsters Meyer Lansky and Mickey Cohen, as well as many others.

All these Americans worked to help the struggling Jewish people in the Land of Israel recover from the Holocaust and fashion the rebirth of their ancient homeland.

Most of those who helped, of course, weren't famous or wealthy.

Paul Kaye, for example, had fought the Nazis in Europe. It was 1947, and Kaye, age twenty, lived in the Bronx with his sister. One day in the music store where he worked, he received a mysterious call. The voice on the phone asked him if he wanted to help the Jewish people. Kaye had been a marine engineer for the U.S. Navy and was curious about what the man wanted. The voice continued, "If you want to help your people, be on the corner of Thirty-Ninth Street and Lexington Avenue on the southeast side on Thursday afternoon at four o'clock. A man with a black leather jacket will walk by. If he puts a newspaper under his arm, follow him. If he puts it in a wastepaper basket, walk away because you're being followed." Click. The call ended.

Kaye was on the corner at the right time. A man in a black leather jacket walked by with a paper under his arm. Kaye followed him around the corner into the Students Lounge used by young people from the Land of Israel.

Kaye asked the man why he had called. The man said he was from the Haganah. Kaye had heard about the Jewish paramilitary organization that defended the Jews in Palestine. The man noted that many of the Jews who had survived the Nazis had no home and wished to enter the Land of Israel. The British, however, had a strict quota and prevented entry, moving the Jews they caught to barbed-wire camps on Cyprus. The Haganah wanted Kaye to help take the refugees to Palestine on small boats and break through the British naval blockade.

The man then stared at Kaye. "The British will hang you if they catch you."

Kaye stared right back.

"Let's go," he said.

The heroic stories of Paul Kaye and others like him are inadequately known. Kaye was one of about 250 daring and resourceful American veterans who tried to help Holocaust survivors get past the British blockade and return to their ancient homeland.

But those veterans were part of a wider effort by Americans between the end of World War II in 1945 and the birth of Israel in 1948 to do whatever was needed so that Israel would survive its very birth. There were efforts conducted in public. But often these Americans, like Paul Kaye, skirted or broke the law as they saved the dream of national Jewish rebirth. There was, for example, an American embargo on selling arms to the emerging Jewish nation, but without such arms the new nation would not survive the coming attack by multiple Arab nations.

In *Americans and the Birth of Israel*, I tell at least part of the dramatic story of the rebirth of Israel. The story of the Jewish return to their homeland takes place over almost two thousand years. It started when the Jews left or were forced out after the Romans conquered the land and the Jews lost their Second Temple in 70 CE and then lost a final war with the Romans in 135 CE. After that, the Jewish connection to the Land of Israel was tenuous. Jews still lived there. Many traveled there to visit or pray or die.

It was not until 1897, when the Viennese playwright Theodor Herzl organized the First Zionist Congress and the political effort to reestablish a Jewish nation found an institutional structure, that a successful conclusion was reached.

But if Jews wanted a nation, there were innumerable impediments. Most important, the land itself was controlled by Turkey. Then in 1917, Britain gained control of the land during the First World War.

Beyond control of the land, there was another important issue. While many Jews lived on the land and more came to stay, Arab Muslims and Christians lived there and also claimed the land as their own.

Meanwhile, the Jews in Europe were facing a horrific nightmare. The Nazis in Germany started the Second World War in 1939, and as one of their explicit aims, they sought to murder every Jew in Europe. Six million Jews eventually died. Many of the survivors felt they needed a refuge, a place to recover, and a new beginning. They looked to their ancient homeland and the new Zionist efforts for that recovery.

The British eventually decided to leave that ancient Jewish homeland, turning the issue of the disputed land over to the United Nations. In 1947, the United Nations voted to divide the land into two nations, one Arab and the other Jewish.

The Arabs and some Jews didn't like the idea of partition. When the British left in May 1948, the Jews declared independence and the surrounding Arab nations combined to attack the new nation of Israel.

The Jews of Israel were few. They lacked weapons. They had no planes. As early as 1945, the Jews in the Land of Israel realized that if they were going to survive, they could not do it on their own. They desperately needed help.

That help came from all over the world. Jews and Gentiles, many reacting to the Holocaust, helped.

But it was to America that the Zionists turned, for only America had the necessary resources. It was America that would provide the money and materials, as well as the people, that aided Israel in its most desperate hour.

This book tells the story of how a ragtag group of Americans of all religions worked—most often in secret and facing the possibility of arrest and imprisonment—to make sure that after the Holocaust, a refuge for Jews would be born. It is a story that deserves to be told. In my mind, it is a story that deserves to be shouted.

This book tells the story of how Americans raised money; gathered munitions, ships, and planes; rescued Holocaust survivors and sneaked them past the British patrols; helped Israel prepare militarily; engaged in dramatic political efforts in Washington, DC, and the United Nations to secure Israeli statehood; participated in cultural activities to support the Zionist cause; and in many other ways made a decisive difference in allowing Israel to be born.

Americans sometimes worked with agents of the Haganah and the Irgun, the Haganah's rival, which was often called a terrorist organization. The agents from Israel had no choice. They were desperate, and their leaders knew that America was the only place they could get what they needed to survive. Together, the Jews from the West and the Jews from the East struggled to obtain what was needed before the Arab armies attacked Israel. In the end, it was the success of the American operation that allowed Israel to live.

This book will, for example, tell the story of:

Rudolf Sonneborn, an oil executive who secretly organized the key American group of wealthy American Jews, known as the Sonneborn Institute, to find whatever was needed in any way necessary.

Golda Meyerson (who would later change her name to Golda Meir), the American from Milwaukee who had moved to the Land of Israel and who, in Israel's crucial time of need, knew what to do. She defied David Ben-Gurion, the leader of the Jewish community in the Land of Israel, and forced the cabinet to overrule him so that she might go to America to raise money. There was a hope that $5 million might be raised, even though everyone assumed that such a staggering sum could not be reached. In fact, the Jewish leaders really needed between $25 and $30 million. These leaders didn't figure on Meyerson, however. Starting in Chicago and speaking before a non-Zionist group of Jews, she told the audience that the Zionists had already made the decision to fight. The one-time schoolteacher then continued, telling the audience that they would have to make a decision as well. They would have to decide whether the Jews or the Arabs would win the fight. Meyerson stayed in America for six weeks, traveling and speaking. In the end, she returned home not with $5 million but with $50 million.

Teddy Kollek, then a Haganah agent and later the famed mayor of Jerusalem, who approached William Levitt, the builder of Levittown. Meeting at Levitt's office in Manhasset, Kollek had to be careful with his words. "We need money," Kollek said. "I can't tell you what it's for, but if you lend us the money, the provisional government of the State of Israel will give you a note and pay you back in a year." Kollek couldn't say that the money was needed to purchase weapons, but Levitt understood. Kollek then asked Levitt for $1 million. There was no collateral, no interest, and, indeed, no clear certainty that the money would ever be returned. Levitt immediately gave him the funds.

American sailors like Paul Kaye, who together saved over thirty-two thousand refugees from the Nazis. This group was made famous in Leon Uris's novel *Exodus* and the movie adapted from the book, starring Paul Newman.

David "Mickey" Marcus (as portrayed by Kirk Douglas in the film *Cast a Giant Shadow*), who helped Israel prepare militarily for the War of Independence.

Ordinary Americans like Eddie Jacobson, who happened to be President Harry S. Truman's former business partner and who walked into the White House to confront his best friend about the Land of Israel at a vitally crucial moment.

People behind the scenes in the White House and around the country who worked feverishly as the United Nations was voting to decide whether a Jewish nation would ever come into being.

The American women's Zionist group Hadassah, whose leaders and members saved abandoned Jewish children, mostly orphans, and brought them to the Land of Israel.

Jewish gangsters, proud that Jews were willing to fight.

Celebrities such as those listed above. For example, the great actor Marlon Brando took part in a play meant to support the Jewish effort to form a nation. Frank Sinatra was among many celebrities who provided money to help the Jews.

In addition to telling the story of how these Americans contributed to Israel's birth, this book will deal with serious underlying issues, such as the story's pertinence to today's world. In particular, the book will deal with the relationship between American and Israeli Jews in all its complexity. For example, on the surface it appears that some small number of American Jews simply violated American law in order to help Israel emerge. Even now, some Arab supporters charge that the American Jews were guilty of dual loyalty. But in fact, these Jews found deep sympathy among many American officials. The complex nature of legal matters, of the role these American Jews found themselves playing during a traumatic post-Holocaust era, needs to be part of this story, as Americans continue to be engaged in an ongoing effort to define the nature of their relationship to Israel, their attachment to it, the ways they should express their differences with it, and the ways they can understand themselves as pro-American and pro-Israeli.

The overall story told in this book is complicated because the action occurred over several years and so much was happening in so many places at the same time. To tell the story in a strict chronological order, which is how I usually proceed, would prompt even more confusion. Instead, I tried to divide up the story into more manageable parts, but even so the tale requires alert readers. To help, I have offered a list of some of the key people in the book as a reference. The very confusion, the very complications, turn out to be an accurate reflection of the reality of what happened. Few people had more knowledge about the events than what actions they themselves took. To try to get a complete overview, as I attempt in this book, would be like trying to tell the whole story of a war in a single brief volume. Still, individual stories show a kind of heroism that is stirring, and if it sometimes seems like a challenge to follow each step of what is going on, I suggest focusing on the separate, individual stories as they appear. They are enough to provide the flavor of an extraordinary and secret adventure.

I begin the book where the story began, in an apartment in New York in 1945. Then I jump chronologically to the vote at the United Nations in order to understand the crucial political event that set up the conflict and explains the need for arms in the Jewish state after the British left. After that, I go back and tell the story of the different efforts on behalf of Israel.

Various decisions had to be made in the writing of the book. Some of the knottiest decisions have to do with language. As I noted in my book *The Dream of Zion: The Story of the First Zionist Congress*, Arabs and Israelis fight over borders and hills, over stones and words.

Since the book is specifically about a Jewish enterprise in history, I will use BCE (Before the Common Era) instead of BC and CE (Common Era) instead of AD.

The designation of the land under discussion is a much more complex question. There are evasive ways to avoid the problem, but they are misleading. For that reason, I have decided against calling it "the Promised Land." This term obviously carries with it both theological and political freight and is more a political than useful term. Jews did not normally refer to the land as the "Holy Land." It is therefore inaccurate to use such a term in describing a Jewish effort.

The name "Palestine" is the most contentious and confusing contender as a name for the land discussed here. Prior to the Jewish revolt led by Bar Kochba against the Roman Empire in 135 CE, the Jews, the Romans, and others referred to the land as "Judea" and "Galilee." The Emperor Hadrian, however, vindictively sought to celebrate his victory and punish the defeated Jewish people. He did this in part by deciding to rename the land, calling it Palestine for the first time. The name Palestine was deliberately chosen because it derived from the Philistines, the people well known as the enemies of the Jews. Hadrian sought to taunt the conquered Jews by renaming the land after their historical opponents.

The name Palestine later ceased to be used. It was revived when the British applied it again, beginning in the nineteenth century, as an imprecise geographic term. The name was imprecise because there never was, in all of human history, a nation called Palestine, so there were no borders that could be defined. Palestine was a useful and neutral term for many years, even though it derived from a non-Jewish, or more accurately, an anti-Jewish, source. But it was a widely used and widely understood term. As part of the Ottoman Empire, it had its own governmental designation, but even that wasn't always clear.

After the First World War, the British tried to be more precise in designating the territory but then gave a substantial part of it to create the nation of Transjordan, later called Jordan. Currently, the term is used in a very explicitly political way by Arabs who live in the territory west of the Jordan River. Ironically, the term *Palestinian* for many years referred to the Jews living in the land, so it is more linguistically accurate to differentiate the peoples as *Palestinian Arabs* and *Palestinian Jews*. The use of the term *Palestinian* simply to describe the Arab population, however historically misleading, is by now very widespread.

The term *Palestine* is not rooted in the Jewish past and as a result is not the most precise term to use in a story about the attempt to revive that past Jewish homeland. However, Jews did use it for many years simply because it was used by others.

There are political implications in continuing to use this term. To call the land Palestine is historically accurate, for when the Jews were planning to create their state in Palestine the term's neutrality was clear to all; whereas today, to use the term *Palestine* is inadvertently to hint that there once was a Palestinian Arab nation on the land that the Jews usurped. The political freight carried by the name Palestine therefore makes it an unhelpful term.

Within the Jewish community, the Jewish people knew the country as Eretz Yisrael, the Land of Israel. But as a historical term used during the era under discussion, roughly 1945 to 1948, the term *Palestine* meant the Jewish people living in the Land of Israel. I will therefore use both terms, trying to distinguish them as best I can.

But even giving the land a name doesn't end the problem. The geographic contours of the Land of Israel are also unclear. Part of this problem is that there was no specific political entity called Palestine before or under the Ottoman Empire. Without defined borders, the Zionist aspirations could not be clearly stated, and that fact has created problems that continue until the present.

And so, burdened by the insights and drawbacks of ideology, by the promise and limitations of language, by the weight of numerous but conflicting testimonies, I offer what I believe is an accurate portrayal of what happened at the birth of Israel and how Americans made contributions that in fact were indispensable to Israel's miraculous reappearance and the return of the Jewish people to national history.

I

THE SECRET MEETING

The small, stubby man with tufts of white hair separated by a space of leathery baldness knew the meeting would help determine the fate of the Jewish people. As he hurried through the lobby of Hotel Fourteen at 14 East Sixtieth Street and out into the blistering heat of New York City's streets, he could feel the burden he carried. He knew many Jews had been killed in Europe, but he didn't know the number, that there were six million victims, a million and a half of whom were children. He knew the fate of the Jews of the Land of Israel might rest on his shoulders. Never had history felt so heavy.

It was July 1, 1945. The year had already been filled with dramatic events. Franklin D. Roosevelt died on April 12. On April 27, Benito Mussolini, the fascist leader of Italy, was shot, and his corpse was hung upside down on meat hooks from the roof of a gas station. Three days later, on April 30, Adolf Hitler, facing defeat and long-overdue justice, bit down on a cyanide capsule as he shot and killed himself. His body was put in a bomb crater, covered with gasoline, and set afire so that the charging Red Army could not retrieve his remains.

For European Jews, 1945 was both a nightmarish and a hopeful year. It was, at its beginning, still death drenched and, at its conclusion, filled both with freedom and the awful realization of the scope of the genocide that the Nazis had undertaken with such ferocity. Anne Frank died in March. On April 4, a concentration camp in Ohrdruf, Germany, became the first liberated by American troops. On April 11, Buchenwald was liberated. Bergen-Belsen was liberated on April 15. Battle-hardened American troops broke down in tears as they saw the prisoners in the camps. For Jews, the news, the photos, and the film that emerged provided a life-altering shock. They were furious that the world had let such mass murder happen in the twentieth century. Some felt, incorrectly, that the victims had not fought back enough. Some felt guilty at their own ignorance and powerlessness during the horror. The whirlwind of emotions provided many Jews, especially those living in Palestine, with a vivid reminder of what life without a nation could lead to, coupled with a steely and unyielding determination to save the refugees and to build a refuge from future persecution, to create a new Jewish homeland—whatever the sacrifices they might have to make.

Ordinary Americans in 1945 were relieved that the decades of the Great Depression and World War II were finally over. Soldiers came home, got married, and had children. A new house cost $4,600, and even though the average wage was $2,400 a year, returning vets bought those homes, especially in the suburbs. They paid fifteen cents for a gallon of gas in the newly built gas stations as they drove to their jobs. Bess Myerson, a Jewish woman, was crowned Miss America. America seemed ready to start a new life despite some labor strikes and the emergence of the Soviet Union as a rival and potential enemy.

David Ben-Gurion, the man headed to that July 1 meeting, had all this and more on his mind. He chaired the Executive Committee of the Jewish Agency for Palestine. As such, he was the de facto leader of the Jewish community in the Land of Israel. He was a man with a fire in his veins, a man with the iron will of a Prussian general, a man who, despite his appearance, felt himself astride a very uncooperative beast of fate.

Ben-Gurion was blessed, or cursed, with an uncanny ability to fast-forward history in his mind. He had a sixth sense of seeing around the corners to determine where events were going, but he lacked the ability to convince all his colleagues of the accuracy of his vision. Many of his own supporters in the Land of Israel found it painfully difficult to accept the scope of the genocide as its full horrors unfolded before the world. These were idealists, grounded in an inherent sense of progress and justice, believers in democracy, and as such convinced that the United Kingdom and the other victorious Allies would help the suffering survivors. American Jews he met were adamantly unwilling to risk what they continued to regard as their precarious place in American society.

Ben-Gurion had recently visited the displaced persons camps and then flown to London in March 1945 to argue for increased immigration to Palestine and to attend a meeting of the Zionist Political Committee.

That effort for increased immigration was not going well. On May 22, 1945, Chaim Weizmann, the leader of Zionism in the British Empire and the man who would become Israel's first president, wrote to Prime Minister Winston Churchill asking him to revoke the White Paper of 1939, which severely limited Jewish immigration to the Land of Israel. Weizmann noted that the restrictions were "prolonging the agony of the Jewish survivors" of the Holocaust. Churchill responded on June 9, saying the restrictions couldn't be considered until all the Allies were at a peace table.

Churchill's response was discussed at a meeting on June 13. Ben-Gurion was particularly upset. He originally had wanted two million Jews to come to Palestine and now had reduced that figure to one million. (In fact, although Ben-Gurion was not yet aware of this, only one million non-Russian European Jews had survived the Nazi onslaught.) Ben-Gurion's despair was deepened by a report that President Franklin Roosevelt had met King Ibn Saud of Saudi Arabia after the Yalta Conference in early February and had promised him not to undertake any actions that the Arabs would consider hostile.

Feeling trapped and losing optimism, Ben-Gurion made a fateful decision, the kind leaders sometimes had to make, however difficult or, in this case, even impossible the decision seemed to be.

Ben-Gurion knew he needed money and weapons. Either he would have to fight the British the way his enemies in the Irgun proposed or the British would leave and he would have to fight the Arabs. The Irgun were Ben-Gurion's political enemies, a group that was more militant than the mainstream Jewish organization Ben-Gurion headed, more willing to fight the British.

The Jews had enough fighters and arms to stop the local Palestinian Arabs, but those fighters were completely unprepared to take on well-trained and well-armed Arab armies. Whatever happened, a deeply worried Ben-Gurion needed support, and a lot of it. Gloomily, he realized that only Zionist supporters in America had the means to save the dream of a Jewish nation reborn.

Ben-Gurion was a man of action. He sent Reuven Shiloah (then still known as Reuven Zaslani) to America. Shiloah was an intelligence expert who would later be the director of the Mossad. Shiloah had a single task: determine whether the existing Zionist organizations in the United States would provide more than financial support. That is, would these American Zionists gather the weapons and all else that the Jews needed in order to fight?

Shiloah soon learned that the existing organization would not engage in potentially illegal actions in order to arm the Jews in the Land of Israel. The American Jewish leadership made it clear that they would engage in no illegal activities. Some didn't think the Jews needed weapons. Without exception, they dismissed the possibility of smuggling weapons, of acting in any way that put their loyalty to the United States in question.

It was then that Ben-Gurion decided to visit the United States himself, to figure out a way around existing organizations. Ben-Gurion was a gruff and tough leader. Although he was deeply learned and revered scholars, Ben-Gurion had no time for intellectuals trying to act as though they were political leaders. He would never say it, but it is likely that Ben-Gurion thought American Jewish leaders dangerously naive, incapable of understanding the realities of life in the Land of Israel or what it took to survive in its hostile neighborhood.

Ben-Gurion arrived in America vowing to make the American Jewish leaders, including the American Zionist leaders, understand his vision. But he was wrong. The first Zionists he approached disagreed about the need for weapons at all.

Undeterred—a word that summarizes his entire life—Ben-Gurion vowed to find another way. There had to be some American Jews, maybe not leaders but hardheaded practical people, who understood the dangers Jews faced, who understood that after the Holocaust, a Jewish nation was the only way Jews could survive. Ben-Gurion went to the informal Haganah headquarters in New York. It was the Haganah, the paramilitary organization that would eventually evolve into the Israeli Army, that was charged with defending the Jewish community. The Haganah's headquarters was at the Hotel Fourteen. Once he was settled in his room, Ben-Gurion summoned Meyer Weisgal, an American journalist, activist, first head of the Zionist Organization of America, and someone who had the necessary connections to wealthy American Jews.

Ben-Gurion, lying on his bed, spent three hours describing the Jews' situation. If the Jewish community could get the refugees, they would have enough fighters to ward off an Arab attack. But even with those soldiers, there was a woeful lack of money and weapons. That, he told Weisgal, was why he had come to America.

Weisgal had never heard the situation sketched so clearly. Whatever other American Zionists might think, Weisgal thought Ben-Gurion's vision was frighteningly real. Weisgal put Ben-Gurion in touch with Henry Montor, the head of the United Jewish Appeal. Ben-Gurion and Montor met on June 25. Listening to Ben-Gurion's urgent analysis, Montor called Rudolf Sonneborn, a wealthy oil executive.

Sonneborn was tall and handsome. He had played football at Johns Hopkins and flew for the U.S. Navy during the First World War. From January to August 1919, Sonneborn, who turned twenty-one during this time, visited Palestine. At the suggestion of a friend of the family, the eminent U.S. Supreme Court justice Louis D. Brandeis, Sonneborn had attended the Paris Peace Conference as secretary to a Zionist delegation from America. It was after the conference that Sonneborn visited Palestine. He wanted to decide whether it was indeed possible to create a Jewish state in his people's ancient homeland. Sonneborn's impressions of his journey are preserved in forty-four letters he sent home. Fatefully, it was on this trip that Sonneborn met and became friends with David Ben-Gurion. The tall American capitalist and the short socialist from the Land of Israel saw in each other the sort of person who acted and didn't just talk, who understood the role of a leader.

And now that friendship was going to be renewed. On Monday, June 26, Ben-Gurion met Sonneborn in the El Patio Room at the Hotel McAlpin. Ben-Gurion was blunt about the Jews' situation. Sonneborn asked if the Jews could defend themselves if fighting came. Ben-Gurion responded, "No. That is why I am here."

Sonneborn, working with Montor, drew up a list. The people on the list were Jewish, hardheaded, wealthy, and, crucially, could keep a secret. They were not the richest, the most famous, or the most influential Jews in America, but they were the ones handpicked for a particularly delicate mission. These were men who not only would be called on to donate funds and organize others, but they would also be risking their reputations. It was even possible that they would face legal prosecution and end up in prison.

With the names in hand, Sonneborn began calling each man he had listed. The men were invited to a meeting at Sonneborn's penthouse home at 455 East Fifty-Seventh Street in New York in just a few days, on Sunday, July 1. The short time between the call and the meeting was meant to preserve secrecy as much as possible. Sonneborn told the men that the meeting was private and could not be discussed with anyone. Jewish leaders from Palestine would be there for an off-the-record discussion of the *Yishuv*, the Jewish community in the land in which they hoped to reestablish a Jewish state. Most of those called said they hoped to attend. Sonneborn immediately wrote letters to all those he had called.

Sonneborn couldn't sleep well during the night before the meeting. Finally, at six in the morning, realizing that any more rest was going to elude him, Sonneborn began his day. He showered, had coffee and bagels, and began to worry. He wasn't sure how many people would really attend or how interested they would be in what Ben-Gurion had to say.

David Ben-Gurion made his way toward Sonneborn's home. The heat was overwhelming. Fifty thousand New Yorkers had slept on the beaches the night before.

Ben-Gurion wondered if the devilish heat was an omen. Would its oppressive nature keep people from attending or listening or caring? He wiped the sweat from his face and kept walking.

Finally, he reached Sonneborn's building. Ben-Gurion walked through Sonneborn's door. The walls of the apartment were dark green with white paneling. The living room had high ceilings, and chairs had been carefully arranged so the guests could speak with each other.

The meeting was set for 9:30 a.m. Sonneborn had written that they would conclude by 4:30 or 5:00 p.m. The nervous Sonneborn was relieved each time his doorbell rang. All the men he had invited showed up.

There are various accounts of exactly who attended the meeting. One standard version is that besides Sonneborn and Montor, there were sixteen other Americans present. They were joined by three representatives from Palestine—David Ben-Gurion; Eliezer Kaplan, the treasurer of the Jewish Agency; and Reuven Shiloah, as well as Meyer Weisgal.

Weisgal was there as a representative of Chaim Weizmann, president of the World Zionist Organization. In that position, Weizmann was the diplomatic representative of the Jewish people to world leaders. Because of his role, Weizmann had to remain unconnected to armed struggles. As did the fiery and brilliant Rabbi Abba Hillel Silver, president of the Zionist Organization of America. Like Weizmann, he was a representative of the Jewish people, in his case American Jews, and so he too had to operate in a way that was completely legal. It was this dilemma of needing to maintain diplomatic contacts and still prepare for armed conflict that drove Ben-Gurion to seek a group outside the normal circles, a group that could have a less scrupulous relationship with the legalities of their enterprise.

Ben-Gurion sat as he began to talk in his heavily accented English to the invited guests in Rudolf Sonneborn's apartment. No notes were kept of the meeting, but there were various later recollections.

Ben-Gurion looked around the room. He knew these were good people, caring Jews, and so he started with a blunt question: "Would America take in many thousands of the displaced European refugees?" These men had lived through an intense era of American anti-Semitism and knew firsthand how reluctant Americans had been to enter the war in Europe. They knew perfectly well that America was not going to let in the Jewish refugees. Ben-Gurion also knew all this, and so he didn't wait for an answer. Only the Jews in Palestine wanted and needed these refugees, he said. But the British, who controlled the land, would not allow more than a few to enter. They did not wish to anger the local Arabs, and they feared more Jews would result in an open revolt against British rule.

Eventually, the prophetic Ben-Gurion emerged. He told the assembled group that the British would give up their mandate over Palestine, and when that happened the remaining Jews would be left alone to fight the invading Arab armies. It is not clear if Ben-Gurion believed this or if he thought American Jews would not help if the arms they would help acquire would be used in an armed revolt against continuing British rule. Whether it was a tactical decision to omit mention of having to fight the British or whether Ben-Gurion truly believed the British would give up the mandate, he was careful that morning to frame the argument as one of Jews all alone against overwhelming Arab numbers. He said the British would give up their mandate in "two or three years." (They eventually gave up the mandate in two years. Ben-Gurion's gift or curse proved right again.)

Ben-Gurion pushed the logic of his argument to the next step. In order to fight the Arabs, the Jews would need all kinds of weapons they didn't have. Only American Jews were in a position to provide some of these weapons and the money to obtain more.

The men in the room were slowly grasping the enormity and significance of the task they were being called on to undertake. One of them wanted to know if there was an alternative to the vision Ben-Gurion had laid out. No, Ben-Gurion said. The British will leave, and we must declare a state. If Jews were to have that Jewish state, they needed a majority in the area that would be allocated to them. This would happen when the Jewish refugees entered the homeland. That was another piece of the puzzle of survival. The Jews would have to break through the British lines blocking entry. And they would. Ben-Gurion acknowledged that the declaration of a Jewish state would mean war. There was no alternative. The Jews would have to resist the invading Arab armies, and those brave Jews desperately needed weapons with which to fight.

Ben-Gurion pressed on, linking the fates of American Jews and those living in the Land of Israel. The men present had at least an elementary knowledge of the Zionist movement and modern history. Now they were being asked to walk into that history. Some must have had mixed feelings. After all, every one of them led comfortable American lives. At any moment, if they chose to do so, they could have assimilated completely into the surrounding society. Ben-Gurion was leading them slowly, but these were highly intelligent men. It is likely that they understood the implications of what they might be called on to do. They were risking their fate to help Jews living in a far-off land.

It was ninety-seven degrees outside. Ben-Gurion took a sip of water. The men in the room smoked or drank Coca-Cola or ginger ale. Just after noon, a spread of cold meats and cheeses, salad, and iced tea was provided for the guests.

Ben-Gurion no doubt wondered if those assembled understood they were at a gateway. If they walked through, the Jews of the Land of Israel might live. If they stayed and did not participate, those same Jews were in danger of facing a second slaughter in a decade.

Shepard Broad, a Miami Beach attorney, had a question: What, exactly were the Jews of the *Yishuv* like? Ben-Gurion said the Jews in the Land of Israel were like Iowa farmers. If some stranger came by seeking food and water, the farmer would invite the stranger inside and provide what was needed. But if a stranger knocked and told the farmer to get off his land right away, why then the farmer would come back to the door holding a shotgun.

And just where would these needed armaments come from? All three Jews from the *Yishuv* answered. The Japanese were on the verge of surrender. As soon as that happened, all kinds of surplus and used weapons, munitions, tents, uniforms, and much else would be available at affordable prices. Eliezer Kaplan, the money expert, went over the costs. Reuven Shiloah discussed how all that was obtained could get to Palestine. Shiloah was no doubt honest. He must have told the men that the goods would have to be smuggled in past the British and against American law. Millions of dollars would be needed for all this.

The questions kept on coming. No one doubted the need. No one expressed any doubts. No one stormed out or quietly claimed that some family concern compelled him to leave.

Ben-Gurion ended by saying that only the American Jews, only those assembled in that room, could save the dream of a revived nation, could save the Jewish refugees, could save those farmers and workers in the Land of Israel. Ben-Gurion told them he depended on them, that he needed to know just how far they were willing to go. He did not ask for a direct commitment, but their presence, their staying, their questions constituted that commitment.

Ben-Gurion asked them to be prepared. When the time came, he would call on them. He asked them again to keep the entire discussion confidential. And as he later recorded in his diary, Ben-Gurion told them that they "should consider yourselves the American arm of the underground Haganah."

There was no doubt left in their minds. They knew what was at stake.

Five of the men agreed to serve as Ben-Gurion's liaisons. Besides Sonneborn, the men included Shepard Broad of Miami, Sam Chorr of New York, Julius Fligelman of Los Angeles, and Harold G. Goldenberg of Minneapolis.

Ben-Gurion recalled in his diary that this "was the best Zionist meeting I had in the United States." Sonneborn later wrote: "We were not given any hint as to what we would be required to do, when we would be required to do it, and who would be the one who would come to tell us what we were required to do. We were simply told to remain ready and to recruit Americans of similar viewpoints to ours."

And so what later was half jokingly and half seriously dubbed "the Sonneborn Institute" was born. The actual term wasn't coined until a few weeks after that July 1 meeting. Sonneborn received a phone call from an unknown man with a British accent. He was the one who asked for the "Sonneborn Institute."

A very pleased David Ben-Gurion left the meeting satisfied that the first crucial step had been taken.

What Ben-Gurion and the members of the newly formed Sonneborn Institute may not have realized is that they were challenging and redefining the traditional role of the American Zionist.

For much of Zionism's early history, the movement was fiercely opposed by, for example, the Reform movement and major organizations, such as the American Jewish Committee, then largely composed of wealthy German Jewish members. Zionism was perceived dangerous because it might imply that American Jews weren't faithful to America, that they had a dual loyalty.

Louis Brandeis developed a brilliant formulation that he applied with his extraordinary leadership skills to lead American Jews toward Zionism. Brandeis, seeing the future Jewish nation still in its formative state, conceived of the reborn Jewish state as an American-style democracy that would exist to save endangered Jews. American Jews, therefore, were simply recalling all the lessons they had learned as good Americans and applying those lessons to the new Jewish state. There was, in Brandeis's view, no need to change American beliefs to support a Jewish nation overseas. There was no dual loyalty. Helping a Jewish nation was philanthropic. It was building on American values and creating a sister democracy.

Brandeis died at the end of 1941, two months before America entered the Second World War. Two rabbis, Stephen Wise and Abba Hillel Silver, were his successors as the leaders of American Zionism.

Wise was deferential, for some alarmingly so, toward President Franklin Roosevelt in a way that adversely affected efforts to rescue Jews during the Holocaust. However accurate or inaccurate such an accusation might be, Wise's calm approach, his ability to work with others, to rely on the connections he built up was starkly at odds with the fiery activism of Abba Hillel Silver. Silver was a Republican, a highly gifted orator, and a tireless organizer. But his abrasive personality offended President Harry S. Truman, among others.

Silver developed a vision of Zionism that was the opposite of Ben-Gurion's. For Silver, the development of a Jewish nation was not *the* central task of the Jewish people. For Ben-Gurion, it was. Silver saw the United States as an equal Zionist partner. Developing a healthy Diaspora life for Jews was, for Silver, a task equal in importance to developing a Jewish homeland. Therefore, according to Silver, there was no dual loyalty possible. Silver, secure in his American Jewish identity, was providing help for a spiritual homeland, not a political one, not one to which he would ever move. As a spiritual center, Silver asserted that a Jewish nation should not be built on fire and blood.

Silver's position was shared by many mainstream Jewish organizations. For example, on September 22, 1948, the American Jewish Committee produced a memorandum, "What Should Be the Attitude and Relationship of American Jewry, and Particularly A.J.C., toward Israel and Its Problems?" Near the beginning of that memorandum were these words:

> The Jews of the United States should recast their outlook and reverse a trend. Many have fallen into the habit of focusing their attention and energies as Jews on Palestine. This habit should cease. Our thoughts, actions and resolutions should not be shaped by our relation to Palestine, Jewish life in the United States must not be centered around the idea of Israel, its culture or its institutions.

Given such positions, Silver was opposed to the illegal immigration of Jews, the very effort Ben-Gurion was convinced was necessary to save the Holocaust survivors and build up the nation. Ben-Gurion needed Jewish bodies. He needed a Jewish majority. He needed Jewish fighters. Of course, they should study their Bibles. Of course, they had an obligation to the world to redeem it. But before they could undertake any spiritual mission, they had to survive.

Silver didn't want to help Ben-Gurion acquire weapons.

The Brandeis approach and the Silver approach defined American Zionism. Americans didn't have to make aliyah—that is, move to Israel. Their job was to provide economic, political, cultural, and moral support to Israel. They would not surrender their American identities to take on an Israeli identity in which aliyah was a defining life goal, in which knowledge of Hebrew was crucial in order to participate in the Israel conversation, and in which Israel was the senior partner and America a much weaker junior partner.

In the Israeli model championed by Ben-Gurion, there was no equality between Israel and the Diaspora. Israel gave the orders, and the Diaspora listened. This, as Ben-Gurion discovered, was not a model acceptable to mainstream American Jewish leaders.

But Ben-Gurion was stuck. As much as his veins burned with a Zionist fire, he was frustrated that he depended on the British, the Americans, and American Jews.

He had to compromise on his views, and American Jews who would help him gather arms had to compromise on the standard American Zionist model regarding the nature of the relationship between American Jews and Israel.

The American men and women who participated in the gathering of arms and money, sometimes on the edge of the law and sometimes over the edge, were between Silver's and Ben-Gurion's visions of American Zionism.

Their efforts defined that middle ground. And, ironically, it is that middle ground that is crucial in understanding American Jewish life today. Therefore, the activities of the members of the Sonneborn Institute and others deserve close inspection. Their efforts are not simply historical remembrances but end up as guides at the end of their story.

The story, from Ben-Gurion's point of view, got much worse soon after his successful meeting. As if to test the Zionists, the British Labour Party's Clement Attlee defeated Winston Churchill and became the new prime minister. The new foreign secretary, Ernest Bevin, took control of foreign policy on July 27 and was adamantly against admitting the one hundred thousand survivors then in displaced persons camps in the American and British zones in Germany. Bevin would not let the Jewish survivors of the Holocaust be admitted to the Land of Israel. He was also opposed to a Jewish majority or a Jewish state in Palestine.

Bevin had decided to revive the British economy through the acquisition of Arab oil and believed that fifteen hundred Jews a month should be admitted to Palestine, a figure deliberately meant to retain an Arab majority and hamper any Zionist efforts toward statehood. On September 5, Britain officially restricted Jewish immigration to those fifteen hundred people each month.

All this deepened Ben-Gurion's shock.

Having set his American group in place, he now desperately needed someone who was an expert in armaments to come to the United States, recruit volunteers, and begin the arduous task of collecting what was needed, of traveling from idea to reality.

It was time for those who wanted a Jewish state that could survive to start organizing in America in order to build that nation. History had been unbearably cruel to the Jews. It was time for the Jews to fight back.

2

THE UNITED NATIONS AND THE WHITE HOUSE

The Vote for Partition

Because this book is not proceeding in chronological order, the discussion in this chapter will be about events that focus on the 1947 United Nations vote for partition. This story will provide the context for what happened before and after in the effort by many to provide help for the rebirth of a Jewish nation. We start with a bit of historical background.

For four hundred years, from 1517 to 1917, Palestine was under the control of the Ottoman Empire. That is, Palestine was never an independent country, and so, for example, there was never an Arab nation called Palestine. The land had been ruled by several empires since there last had been a Jewish nation in the area. In 1917, the Ottoman Empire lost its lands to various nations, including the United Kingdom. The empire's former land was under the legal control of the League of Nations which, under the 1923 Palestine Mandate, gave Palestine to the British. Once the mandate was established, the British reaffirmed a policy established during World War I in the 1917 Balfour Declaration that asserted British support for a Jewish national home in Palestine. The Arab dismay with this promise kept the land in semipermanent turmoil.

The Arabs in Palestine began a general strike in 1937. (Ironically, when the term *Palestinian* was used in the 1930s and 1940s, it referred to the Jews. The historically accurate language would be to discuss Palestinian Arabs and Palestinian Jews rather than for *Palestinian* to refer exclusively to Arabs. But the Arab population seems to have won this battle in the language war.) The goal of the strike was the establishment of an Arab national home.

The beleaguered British established the Peel Commission, or more formally, the Palestine Royal Commission, in response to the strike. The commission issued a report on July 7, 1937, and concluded what was obvious to everyone on the ground: the continuing British Mandate could not be sustained. Lord Peel, who chaired the commission that bore his name, led discussions that ended in a recommendation that the land be divided into two states, one for the Jews and one for the Arabs. Some Jews opposed this plan, but David Ben-Gurion, perhaps with an eye on the Nazis, who had already come to power in Germany but who had not yet launched World War II, believed forces hostile to the Jews posed such a danger that the Jews should accept much less land than they had been promised. Ben-Gurion may have simply sought a compromise with the Arabs and believed that partition was the clearest path to justice. In any case, the Arabs uniformly refused to discuss partition and would not accept that any land be apportioned for a Jewish nation. Once the Peel Commission report was issued, the British appointed members to the Woodhead Commission to consider the Peel plan in detail and provide practical recommendations for the implementation of a partition. The ensuing recommendation was that an Arab state be linked to Transjordan, the new Arab state the British had created in eastern Palestine on land the Jews had thought they were going to get. The commission also recommended a relatively small Jewish state and a zone for the mandatory authority. The British, through hard-earned experience, understood that the Arabs living in what would become the Jewish state and the Jews living in what would become the Arab state would have problems. Under the partition plan, the commission recommended transferring 225,000 Arabs from the new Jewish state and

1,250 Jews from the new Arab state. Additionally, the commission recommended allowing continued Jewish immigration.

With a total and unanimous Arab rejection of the plan, partition was put aside, especially as the new world war loomed ever closer.

Once the war had ended and the world reacted in horror to the revelations about the scope of the Holocaust and the unbearably grisly nature of Nazi torture and murder, there was tremendous sympathy for the plight of the Jews and a widespread recognition of the urgent need for a Jewish state to provide a haven for the Holocaust survivors and a safe place for a Jewish future. It is inaccurate to see the Holocaust as the cause of the birth of a Jewish state because by that point, the Zionist movement had been active for fifty years, but certainly revulsion at what had happened made the Zionist case as clear as possible. It was when Allied armies entered the Buchenwald concentration camp on April 11, 1945, that Americans saw for the first time that the horrible rumors that had seemed so impossible to believe were in fact understatements of the Nazi atrocities. Four days later, Bergen-Belsen was liberated, and then on April 29, the Allies reached Dachau. CBS correspondent Edward R. Murrow was with the American army. So overwhelmed were the soldiers and Murrow, so unbelievable were the sights, that Murrow began his report about the event with the words, "I pray that you will believe me."

In August 1945, President Harry S. Truman strongly requested that the British admit one hundred thousand survivors of the Holocaust into Palestine, but the British, who had issued a white paper in 1939 that severely limited Jewish immigration, refused to lift the restrictions. The United States continued to apply pressure. The Jews in the Land of Israel continued to attack the British soldiers and military installations.

The effect of all this was to heighten British antipathy toward their own mandate. Despite the Peel Commission's failure, the British established the Anglo-American Committee of Inquiry in November 1945 to devise some sort of political framework for the area of the mandate and, perhaps because of external pressure or humanitarian impulses or a combination of both, provide a haven for Holocaust survivors. The

Zionists thought the Land of Israel had been investigated more than enough; they argued that it was action that was needed. President Truman favored the Anglo-American Committee because he believed that such a committee would inextricably unite the future of the Holocaust survivors and the political status of the Land of Israel. The British, privately of course, were furious with Truman, suggesting that all he cared about was securing Jewish political and economic support.

The twelve members of the Anglo-American Committee heard from Ben-Gurion and others and, to their credit, went to displaced persons camps in order to determine from the survivors themselves where they wished to go. This led to a bit of a high-stakes chess game. Zionists came to the camps before the committee members and "suggested" to the people there that they needed to stress their desire to go to Palestine. British intelligence agents, meanwhile, discovered this effort. In fact, people in the camps needed no pressure from any side. They, virtually unanimously, wanted to go to Palestine, where they knew they were wanted and could be among Jews who understood them. The Americans had not taken them in during the war, and almost no one else had either. A Jewish homeland, in some sense, was not only the desired option but the only realistic one for very large numbers of Jews.

The committee completed its report on April 20, 1946. It recommended that one hundred thousand Jewish refugees from Europe be admitted to Palestine, that the white paper's restrictions on the sale of land to Jews be rescinded, that the country be neither exclusively Jewish nor Arab, and that the British trusteeship over Palestine be extended. The United States approved of the findings concerning immigration and land purchases.

The British surrendered on February 25, 1947. They announced that they were going to terminate the Palestine Mandate and refer the issue to the United Nations, the successor to the League of Nations, which had given them the mandate.

One aspect of this issue that is inadequately discussed is that American Jews were not solidly pro-Zionist. The British journalist and writer Isaiah Berlin estimated that fully half of America's Jews opposed the idea of a Jewish state. Some American Jews were religious and thought only the Messiah could bring Jews to their Holy Land. A much larger, and more secular, group of American Jews believed that America was their homeland, and they feared being accused of being more loyal to the Jewish nation than to their own or of having divided loyalties. Some feared a Jewish nation would mean perpetual fighting because the Arabs in the region would not accept a Jewish nation. Because of this opposition, President Truman was receiving very mixed messages. His State Department, for example, was adamantly opposed to a Jewish nation.

Certainly, Truman had humanitarian sympathies, but he didn't like the pressure that Jewish groups and leaders put on him. He found Rabbi Abba Hillel Silver, a Republican and therefore also a political opponent, particularly annoying.

Many people looking at Truman thought he simply had political sensibilities and that those sensibilities made him pro-Zionist as a way to attract Jewish votes. That is why it is so important to recall that many American Jews also opposed such a state. There is a different approach to consider without taking away Truman's genuinely good impulses and analytical skills. He wanted to decide the Palestine issue not on the basis of politics but on the basis of doing what was right. Here it is useful to consider some people he admired.

Consider David K. Niles. Niles had worked with President Franklin D. Roosevelt organizing the labor and ethnic minorities so crucial electorally for the Democrats. Truman had asked Niles to stay on. Jewish nationalism had an extraordinary ally in David K. Niles.

Niles was a perpetually shy man and a secretive one. He never told people what he had discussed with Truman, but Niles was destined to play a major role in providing the president with key information and insights.

Niles was a bachelor who traveled to Boston every weekend. He had loved Justine Wise, the daughter of Rabbi Stephen Wise, arguably the most important representative of the Jewish people in American politics. Justine had married someone else, and Niles could not bring himself to love another woman.

Eddie Jacobson, a former business partner of Truman's, also played an important role. (His story is told below.)

Truman was besieged on all sides. His supposed partners, the British, didn't want partition but a binational state with an Arab majority.

In May 1947, the United Nations formed the United Nations Special Committee on Palestine (UNSCOP), which was given the task of reporting on Palestine and recommending appropriate action. The Arab nations refused to cooperate with UNSCOP. The committee was diligent in its efforts. They were particularly interested in learning why the Arabs opposed any Jewish immigration. UNSCOP held hearings in Jerusalem, but the Arab nationalists best able to make their own case would not testify before the committee.

Most of the pro-Zionists who testified were Jews. But the Reverend John Stanley Grauel was particularly effective precisely because he was a Methodist minister rather than a Jew. He made the committee members understand the burdens Jewish refugees faced and their need to go to their ancient homeland. In a unique way, Grauel was able to make the refugees sympathetic to the committee members. Golda Meir, later prime minister of Israel, observed that Grauel's testimony fundamentally altered the hearings and provided much-needed support for the creation of a Jewish nation. Grauel himself was immensely proud of his testimony. As he wrote in his autobiography: "There was great gratification for me in knowing that my eyewitness report was now a matter of record. Inherent in the nature of the relationship between Christians and Jews was the fact that because I was a Christian, in this situation my testimony would be given greater credence than that of a Jewish crew member."

The committee toured displaced persons camps. They personally witnessed the *Exodus 1947* affair.

UNSCOP had a large staff. Despite this, there was a crucially influential member, Ralph Bunche, an African American. He was in charge of organizing travel and the testimonies given. Bunche prepared the agendas and was responsible for assembling the crucial working papers members read. After the British executed five Jews who had rebelled, Bunche arranged for the committee to meet Menachem Begin, the head of the Irgun and future prime minister of Israel. Bunche was overwhelmed by Jewish suffering, and he began to rediscover his own identity as a member of a persecuted minority. From the moment Bunche met the Jews, he was no longer a dispassionate member of the committee. The Zionists had an influential friend.

Bunche was not the only UNSCOP member who was affected. There were eleven members on the committee. When they started their work, three of them can be said to have been sympathetic to Zionism. Their encounter with survivors, with the Jews in Palestine, with history changed the others. By the end of the three-month period of investigation, on September 3, 1947, the committee was ready to report to the U.N. General Assembly. The committee unanimously voted that the British Mandate over Palestine be ended. The British were certainly not opposed to this; they were happy that an outside group was trying to get rid of a problem for them. A minority on the committee voted for a unified Palestine, one state with Arabs and Jews sharing power. The majority of the committee, however, voted to recommend that the land be partitioned into two states, one Jewish and one Arab.

The General Assembly scheduled a vote on the partition. Two-thirds of the nations voting needed to support the motion in order for it to pass. After nearly two thousand years, the possibility of a revived Jewish nation was real. In two millennia, never had the Jews been under so much political pressure. They had suffered hunger, humiliation, torture, forced conversion, and murder, all culminating in the unspeakable horrors of the Holocaust. Now they needed all their strength and their clearest voice.

David K. Niles sent President Truman a memorandum on July 29, 1947. Niles, ever cautious, was trying his best to get Truman to do what Niles believed Truman really wanted, which was to support a Jewish nation. Niles bluntly said that members of Truman's own State Department would not "vigorously" carry out his policies. "But," Niles continued, "your administration, not they, will be held responsible." This was a crucial moment, for Niles was alerting the president that he would have to oppose the State Department himself.

The next crucial step came from a completely unexpected place, the Soviet Union. The Soviets had opposed Zionism, at least since the 1920s, asserting that it was one more example of imperialism. Britain, the United States, and even the Jewish Agency therefore were under the clear assumption that the Soviets would join the Arab states in being adamantly opposed to the creation of a Jewish state.

And yet on May 14, 1947, Andrei Gromyko, a speaker for the Soviets, was at the General Assembly and announced that the Soviet Union understood "the legitimate rights of the Jewish people." He spoke in favor of a unified single state but recognized that in reality, such a state would be difficult to realize. He concluded by saying that therefore partition was an acceptable alternative.

The Soviets were particularly interested in getting the United Kingdom, a powerful potential enemy, out of the region. Therefore, removing the British Mandate was a key Soviet goal. The Soviets also had some hopes that the new Jewish state, headed by an avowed socialist like David Ben-Gurion, might be brought into the Soviet orbit. Indeed, after Gromyko's announcement, the Jewish Agency and the Soviets had many intense meetings, which deeply upset the Americans.

The Arabs, understandably, were opposed to partition. They did not under any circumstances want a Jewish nation on what they considered to be Arab lands. But the Jewish attitude toward partition also was not wholly supportive.

Some on the right, such as Menachem Begin, opposed partition because the land that was to be apportioned for a Jewish homeland was so small compared to what was promised in the Balfour Declaration. Many Jews thought the proposed borders were simply indefensible and that they would not be able to maintain their state. They feared a sequel to the Holocaust. A tiny minority genuinely wanted a binational state and as a result were opposed to a separate Jewish nation. Ben-Gurion faced dissent even in his own Jewish Agency cabinet. When the time came for a vote on accepting the partition, Ben-Gurion was triumphant—by a single vote.

In November 1947, the United Nations consisted of fifty-seven countries. Some of them, the Jewish Agency assumed, would avoid the issue of partition by abstaining or simply not being available for the vote. Those nations would not be counted. Of the remaining nations that did vote, two-thirds would have to approve the resolution for partition. But with the United States and Soviet Union together, the Jewish Agency saw what might have been a unique, and perhaps one-time, opportunity to get world approval for the re-creation of the Jewish nation.

But as it turned out, the simple mathematics involved in such a calculation was not as straightforward as it seemed. All nations would be subject to counterpressures. The Jewish Agency would push for partition, and the Arab nations would uniformly press for a rejection of the proposal.

Even within a delegation, there was often conflict. This was certainly true within the American delegation. The State Department adamantly opposed partition. Pro-Zionist forces frequently attributed this constantly argued position to anti-Semitism. But while that no doubt was part of the issue, State Department officials also genuinely feared that American interests, especially in the area of oil, would be best served by supporting the Arab point of view. The so-called Arabists in the State Department were in favor of a U.N. trusteeship over the land. They couldn't directly contradict their boss, the president of the United States, so they decided to accept Truman's acceptance of partition, which they angrily viewed as purely political motivation to get Jewish votes in the 1948 election. But while formally supporting partition, they planned to make no effort to influence the votes of other nations. This position seemed supportive, but in fact it would have been catastrophic. Without intense American pressure, many nations would abstain or vote against the proposal. Supporters of partition also realized this.

The United Kingdom announced that it would oppose partition. France and China, the other two powerful nations besides the United Kingdom, the Soviet Union, and the United States, remained unclear on their voting plans. The five Arab nations—Saudi Arabia, Iraq, Syria, Lebanon, and Egypt—were joined in their opposition by nations that had very large Muslim populations. These included Pakistan, Iran, and Afghanistan. Other nations were divided. In the White House, David Niles was particularly interested in the Latin American nations. He assumed that if the United States approved U.N. membership for Spain, the Latin American nations would support partition. Such was the nature of the calculations. Both sides were desperate and anxious.

That anxiety for the pro-partition supporters was especially high on Wednesday, November 26, the day before Thanksgiving. The supporters of partition did a count of votes (a very inexact science for so young an organization as the United Nations was then) and concluded that they would lose the vote, which was scheduled to occur at any minute. The actual arithmetic of the vote would be very complicated precisely because nations could easily avoid taking sides by abstaining, and the Arab states had an automatic number of votes against. It was at this minute that the fine art of political manipulation began. Pro-partition supporters from Latin America began making long speeches with the intention of delaying a vote they feared they might lose. The Arabs, angered at the accusatory remarks hurled at them from the General Assembly's floor, then made a huge tactical mistake. Instead of not responding, and thereby allowing time for the vote to take place, the Arabs gave equally long speeches defending their position. Eventually, a recess was called until Friday. The pro-partition forces now had two days to win the necessary votes.

Everyone was called into action. Neither side believed in being subtle. This was a time for bare-knuckled politics. Intense pressure was used by both sides.

The Democratic Party warned Harry Truman that he couldn't lose, that such a loss would endanger the party's coalition, which included both Jewish and Gentile liberals. Truman, as previously noted, intensely disliked pressure from either side. He wanted to make the historically correct and moral choice based on his own lights. Truman blasted what he saw as "unwarranted interference" with his efforts.

The State Department called the White House to complain about the Jewish Agency efforts. There were wild accusations that the agency had bribed a Latin American ambassador.

Truman, however, sought a middle ground. He finally told David Niles that the United States could exert a little pressure to support partition in addition to voting for it.

With both sides looking at the remaining undecided nations, there was agreement that partition would depend on the votes of four of them: the Philippines, Haiti, Greece, and Liberia. On Wednesday, all of these nations had announced their opposition to partition. Niles made the same calculation as the Jewish Agency. "Somehow" (a euphemism for pressure by the United States) three of these nations had to change their view in order for partition to pass.

Niles called the prominent Jewish Supreme Court justice Felix Frankfurter. He rounded up Frank Murphy, another justice. Together, they paid a call on the Philippine ambassador in Washington, DC. Such a visit by two members of the U.S. Supreme Court was extraordinarily unusual and therefore underlined the importance of the visit. Initially, ten members of the U.S. Senate (later joined by other senators) sent a telegram to the president of the Philippines. The message was clear. A vote against partition would have an adverse effect on American-Philippine relations. As it happened, as the vote was taking place, there was a financial aid package for the Philippines pending in Congress.

And there was more. An American named Julius Edelstein was a friend of the Philippine president. Edelstein was then in England. The American embassy there located him at a hotel. It was the middle of the night, but in a life-or-death battle for the history of a people, waking up someone was not of crucial importance. At first, Edelstein protested, but he eventually agreed to call his friend the president, who himself was awakened from an afternoon siesta.

But one more complication arose. Prior to the Wednesday delay, Carlos P. Romulo, the delegate from the Philippines, had announced that "we hold that the issue is primarily moral. The issue is whether the United Nations should accept responsibility for the enforcement of a policy which is clearly repugnant to the valid nationalist aspirations of the people of Palestine. The Philippines Government holds that the United Nations ought not to accept such a responsibility."

Romulo was recalled.

With a new head of the delegation, the Philippines changed its mind and voted in favor of partition.

Liberia, it turned out, had received no pressure from the United States. Because of this, Liberia felt no urgent need to get involved in creating two states. David Niles called an economist friend named Robert Nathan, who understood the African nation. Nathan in turn called the Liberian delegate in New York, where the United Nations was meeting. Nathan gave the delegate a clear warning. Unless Liberia voted for partition, Nathan would have to call a friend of his, the Episcopalian Edward Stettinius Jr., a former secretary of state, and Secretary Stettinius would call his friend Harvey S. Firestone Jr., the head of the tire and rubber company that was crucial for the Liberian economy. Stettinius, however, didn't call Firestone. Instead, he called the Liberian president directly, explaining his interest in the subject.

Liberia voted for partition.

Haiti was another confusing case. On that Wednesday before Thanksgiving, Haiti had said it would oppose partition, but the country's chief delegate said he would vote for it. Niles organized business friends to determine the status of the actual vote. The Jewish Agency contacted someone to send a cable to Haiti's president.

Haiti voted for partition.

And that left Greece. The country desperately needed aid. In this case, the Americans did not guarantee that a vote for partition would ensure that Greece received a large aid package. The Islamic states promised support for aid, provided Greece voted against partition. Niles called Tom Pappas, a friend from Boston who was Greek and had strong business interests in Greece. Pappas lined up support from such people as Spyros Skouras, a motion picture executive. Telegrams were sent to the Greek prime minister, reminding him how the American Jewish community had rallied to provide aid to Greece during the Nazi occupation of the country.

But the current need for aid and the Arab promise of that aid won. Greece voted against partition.

Efforts were made to gain support from other nations as well. Sam Zemurray, the banana king, reportedly made several calls to nations reliant on the banana trade. France in particular was subjected to intense pressure from all sides.

Chaim Weizmann sent a telegram to Leon Blum, the Jewish ex–prime minister of France. Weizmann wondered, "Does France wish to be absent from a moment unfading in the memory of man?" Blum did not wish to be absent. He called Bernard Baruch, a seventy-seven-year-old famous and influential American financier. Baruch's case is a particularly interesting one because although Jewish, he wasn't a Zionist. He had spent a lifetime apart from any Jewish nationalism. And yet the swirl of history lifted Bernard Baruch and carried him along. He picked up his phone and called the French delegate. With a business leader's bluntness, Baruch told the delegate that a vote against partition would mean the end of American aid to France.

France voted for partition.

When the discussions began again on the Friday after Thanksgiving, the arguments and the parliamentary maneuvering were not finished. Accusations flew back and forth across the room. Both sides felt the presence of history and would not let go of their passions. Indian prime minister Jawaharlal Nehru was furious with the effort to form a Jewish state. He accused the Zionists of attempted bribery and issuing death threats against his sister. India voted against partition. Cuba also claimed it had been pressured and voted against partition.

Although this is a record of Zionist efforts, it should be noted that there were incredible counterpressures by those who opposed partition. An Arab Higher Committee official reportedly attempted to bribe one of the delegates at the United Nations. There were reports that the delegate was Russian, although that is not clear.

Beyond bribery, the anti-partition forces also used direct threats. Jamal Husseini, the representative of the Arab Higher Committee at the United Nations, warned, "We will smash the country with our guns and obliterate every place the Jews seek shelter in." Such threats were not dismissed in the State Department of the United States. Within the department, all the Arab resistance was shaped into an argument that any Jewish state could not survive a war against the Arabs, so it was not prudent for the United States to support a Jewish nation. The actual U.N. vote did not soften the State Department's views.

Nuri al-Said, the prime minister of Iraq, was blunt in his dealings with British diplomats, stating that if partition was granted, Jews in Arab nations would no longer be safe. Indeed, the status of Jews in those nations became a focal point for Arab threats. At the twenty-ninth meeting of the Ad Hoc Committee on Palestine on November 24, Muhammad Hussein Heykal Pasha, the head of Egypt's delegation to the General Assembly, said, "The lives of one million Jews in Moslem countries would be jeopardized by the establishment of a Jewish State." He added, "If the U.N. decides to amputate a part of Palestine in order to establish a Jewish State, no force on Earth could prevent blood from flowing there. . . . No force on Earth can confine it to the borders of Palestine itself. . . . Jewish blood will necessarily be shed elsewhere in the Arab world."

In his speech to the General Assembly on Friday, Fadel Jamall, the foreign minister of Iraq, said, "Partition imposed against the will of the majority of the people will jeopardize peace and harmony in the Middle East. Not only the uprising of the Arabs of Palestine is to be expected, but the masses in the Arab world cannot be restrained. The Arab-Jewish relationship in the Arab world will greatly deteriorate. There are more Jews in the Arab world outside of Palestine than there are in Palestine. In Iraq alone, we have about one hundred and fifty thousand Jews who share with Moslems and Christians all the advantages of political and economic rights. Harmony prevails among Moslems, Christians and Jews. But any injustice imposed upon the Arabs of Palestine will disturb the harmony among Jews and non-Jews in Iraq; it will breed inter-religious prejudice and hatred."

The Arab threats weren't over. They threatened an oil embargo and told the United States that they would realign themselves with the Soviet Union.

The vote didn't take place for another day, on Saturday, November 29, 1947. It was just after five in the evening when the voting began. People took out their pencils and notepads. Every vote counted. Siam was absent, so the vote would be taken among the fifty-six nations present. Ten nations abstained. Thirteen nations voted against partition. Thirty-three nations (two more than the two-thirds majority needed) voted in favor of partition.

Jews around the world were stunned. For the first time in almost two thousand years, their declaration at the Passover seders of "Next Year in Jerusalem" seemed possible.

Rabbi Abba Hillel Silver, the leader of the American Zionists, uncharacteristically cried. There was a Zionist rally at Madison Square Garden. Chaim Weizmann left his sickbed in a hotel to speak at the rally. So overwhelmed by emotion was he that the suave Weizmann lapsed into Yiddish.

In Jerusalem, a woman sat alone in her kitchen, pushing her ear against an old radio set with poor reception. She chain-smoked as she recorded each vote on her notepad. Usually accompanied by many political friends, that evening in Jerusalem Golda Meir chose to sit alone.

Kibbutzim in the north of the Land of Israel were ablaze with bonfires. Cafés in Tel Aviv offered free champagne to celebrating customers.

It should be noted that not all Jews were so eager to celebrate. Menachem Begin in his role as the commander of the Irgun issued an Order of the Day: "The Homeland has not been liberated, but mutilated.... Eretz Israel will be restored to the people of Israel. All of it. And forever."

Begin's message is important. Ben-Gurion and the Jewish Agency had accepted partition. The Arabs had uniformly rejected it. But the binary notion of a Jewish acceptance and an Arab rejection, while formally accurate, misread the complexities of the reaction among all Jews. It is easy to see that Arab rejection has simply continued. That is why there have been wars in the Middle East and repeated failed attempts to sign a peace treaty. The Begin position is a clear indication that a combination of Jewish victory in the 1967 Six-Day War, which resulted in the acquisition of the West Bank and Golan Heights (and the Sinai, which Begin himself later returned to Egypt) and the rise of the right with such prime ministers as Begin and Benjamin Netanyahu meant there was a Jewish ideological view as powerful as the Arab opposition to any Jewish state in any part of Palestine, which to this day makes compromise so difficult.

And there is still another aspect of the partition that even then was recognized as potentially causing trouble: the balance of populations in the Jewish and Palestinian states.

David Ben-Gurion spoke to the Central Committee of the Histadrut (the Eretz Yisrael Workers' Party) several days after the United Nations vote to support partition. Ben-Gurion focused on one issue he considered to be crucial but inadequately examined.

> The total population of the Jewish State at the time of its establishment will be about one million, including almost 40% non-Jews. Such a [population] composition does not provide a stable basis for a Jewish State. This [demographic] fact must be viewed in all its clarity and acuteness. With such a [population] composition, there cannot even be absolute certainty that control will remain in the hands of the Jewish majority. . . . There can be no stable and strong Jewish state so long as it has a Jewish majority of only 60%.

Demography continues to be a crucial matter. There might even be said to be a demographic war among Jews and Arabs (along with military, economic, and other types of wars).

In the immediate aftermath of the vote, most people were happy. But not all.

President Truman was pleased with the vote at the United Nations. Not for the first time, he could compare himself to Cyrus the Great, who had through his actions allowed for the rebirth of a Jewish homeland. The heady success misled Truman, who thought that perhaps there could be cooperation in the land between Jews and Arabs.

The Arab nations reacted to the vote with vows to completely eradicate the Jewish state and drive the Jews out of the land. The Arabs who lived in Palestine were led by Haj Amin al-Husseini. He threatened the Zionists with annihilation, as did most Arab nations. Coming only a few years after the horrors of Nazism, such threats were not dismissed by anybody. Many mainstream Zionists thought the Arabs were angry in the moment but that logic would eventually win them over and they would see the fundamental fairness of dividing the land. The Arab Higher Committee called for a three-day general strike in the land. On December 2, an Arab mob armed with knives and clubs attacked a commercial center in Jerusalem. People in the mob attacked Jews walking by and those in the shops.

The British, in keeping with Ernest Bevin's long-held beliefs, declared that partition should not be imposed on the Arabs. Still, the cabinet decided to end the mandate at midnight on May 14, 1948, but Britain would not take part in enforcing the partition. This had the effect of refusing to stop what was thought to be the overwhelming Arab armies.

Despite the excitement, the vote was, in the end, only a vote. As yet, a plan still had to be formulated. And the Arabs weren't waiting for any plans. On the day after the partition vote, Arabs attacked Jewish positions. The State Department was unmoved by the vote, maintaining its view of the "manifest impossibility of implementing the partition of Palestine." On December 5, 1947, the United States banned the sale or shipment of any weapons to the entire area. As earlier discussed, this had the effect of disarming the Jews because the British continued to fulfill their agreements to arm the Arabs. The State Department did all this by slyly going about its business. David Niles, for instance, never even heard of the planned embargo or he would have fought it vigorously.

It had been in January 1947 that President Truman, knowing he faced a difficult election in 1948 and wanting a highly respected leader on his team, called on General George C. Marshall, the army chief of staff during World War II, to become the secretary of state. Marshall was well regarded throughout the country. He was reserved, cool. He told Truman that he had no feelings, "except a few which I reserve for Mrs. Marshall."

Marshall joined his State Department colleagues in pressuring Truman to back away from the United Nations decision on Palestine in favor of a trusteeship. But the Zionists still had friends in the White House. David Niles was informally in charge of rounding up the Jewish vote for the 1948 election. When he had to go on sick leave, the job was given to his superior, Clark Clifford, a man from Missouri who was a brilliant political tactician but, by self-admission, a man who had no understanding of the Middle East. Clifford therefore brought in a friend of Truman's, Max Lowenthal, to help. This group of men made the difference. They saw the political world the same way. They all liked and trusted each other. So it was on March 6, 1948, that Clifford forwarded a memo to Truman with a blunt message: "The policy of the United States must be to support the United Nations settlement of the Palestine issue." Clifford's skills then became obvious as he outlined, step by step, what had to be done in order to accomplish this goal.

The Zionists had a major problem with the partition plan, a problem they hoped President Truman could remedy. The plan had excluded the Negev region, virtually the entire southern area of what would be a Jewish state.

Jewish activists began to work to get Truman's support. Much of this backfired. Abba Hillel Silver had a fiery, confrontational style. Besides being a Republican, his personality and approach were exactly wrong for Truman. Silver arranged for one hundred thousand telegrams to be sent to the White House, evidently thinking they would provide pressure and thereby show his political innocence. Silver was not alone in misunderstanding the byzantine intricacies of Washington politics. A Brooklyn rabbi with good intentions placed a flier on the desks of children in a public school. The father of one of the children worked for the Arabian American oil company. The father sent the letter to the company's vice president, who sent it to a contact at the State Department. And the contact, Loy Henderson, sent it to a friend in the White House who showed it to a furious Harry Truman.

Zionists came to the White House to argue their position. One report, though inaccurate, captures the flavor of Truman. According to this story, Abba Hillel Silver banged his fist on the president's desk. That such a story would circulate and be believed is a good indication of how Truman felt about pressure. Truman eventually ordered his secretary not to set up any more meetings on the subject.

The Zionists believed only one man could speak to Truman. Although he was ill, Chaim Weizmann went to New York's Waldorf Astoria hotel and sought a meeting with the president. But Truman would not meet him.

Frank Goldman, then the president of the influential Jewish group B'nai B'rith, remembered that Truman had a friend from Missouri, someone with whom the president had served during World War I and a former business partner no less. It was the middle of the night, but Goldman picked up the phone and called Eddie Jacobson. It was, in many ways, a strange choice. Jacobson was no Zionist, but like so many other American Jews, he knew when history was calling him. He agreed to help.

On the following day, March 13, 1948, Jacobson flew to Washington and went to see his old friend. It was a Saturday morning, and Jacobson didn't have an appointment. Matthew Connelly, Truman's appointments secretary, begged Jacobson not to talk about Palestine because Truman was so sick of being pressured by everyone on the subject. Jacobson calmly said, "That's what I came to Washington for." Connelly was in a difficult position. He knew that Jacobson was perhaps Truman's oldest friend, someone for whom Truman had genuine affection.

And yet Connelly was supposed to bar people who came to speak about Palestine. Connelly decided to admit Jacobson.

Jacobson went into the office. He saw that Truman looked well. And then, as Jacobson later recalled,

> For a few minutes we discussed our families, my business. . . . I then brought up the Palestine subject. He immediately became tense in appearance, abrupt in speech and very bitter in the words he was throwing my way. In all the years of our friendship he never talked to me in this manner. . . . I argued with him from every possible angle, reminding him of the feelings for Dr. Weizmann which he often expressed to me, telling him that I could not understand why he wouldn't see him; [I] told him that Dr. Weizmann, an old and sick man, had made his long journey to the United States especially to see the President.

Everyone on Truman's staff, and most Americans, would have backed off at this point, overwhelmed to be in the Oval Office in the presence of the president of the United States of America. But Eddie Jacobson, a simple man, knew Harry Truman perhaps better than anyone outside his own family. Jacobson was not going to let go of history.

"The President remained immovable. He replied how disrespectful and how mean certain Jewish leaders had been to him." Jacobson, bred in the Midwest like Truman and, also like him, having more courtly values than some of the louder protesters, was shocked at his friend. "I suddenly found myself thinking that my dear friend . . . was at that moment as close to being an antisemite [sic] as a man could possibly be, and I was shocked that some of our own Jewish leaders should be responsible for Mr. Truman's attitude."

Desperate, Jacobson tried another approach.

> I happened to rest my eyes on a beautiful model statue of Andrew Jackson. . . . I then found myself saying this to the President, almost word for word, "Harry, all your life you have had a hero. You are probably the best read man in America on the life of Andrew Jackson. . . . Well, Harry, I too have a hero, a man I have never met but

who is, I think, the greatest Jew who ever lived. I too have studied his past and I agree with you . . . that he is a gentleman and a great statesman as well. I am talking about Chaim Weizmann. . . . Now you refuse to see him because you were insulted by some of our American Jewish leaders. . . . It doesn't sound like you, Harry."

Jacobson was, to put it politely, exaggerating his admiration of Weizmann. He probably knew very little of the man's history, of his role in getting Britain to issue the Balfour Declaration, and of his other contributions. But Jacobson wasn't lying. He was emotionally and personally injecting himself into Jewish history. And in that moment he did feel close to Weizmann.

Truman's response to his friend was to use his fingers to begin drumming on his desk. Truman then swiveled in his chair and stared out at the Rose Garden. Jacobson later recalled that the silence seemed "like centuries."

Truman swiveled back again, stared straight into Jacobson's eyes, and said, "You win, you bald-headed son of a bitch. I will see him." Jacobson was overwhelmed.

He left the White House, went to a bar in a local hotel, and drank a double bourbon. Such drinking might be normal for some people. But Eddie Jacobson had never done such a thing in his life.

Weizmann got on a train to Washington, traveling by himself. He arrived on March 18. Truman wanted the meeting to be a total secret, which on one level made sense, but the fact that the president never informed the State Department would soon create a major mess. Weizmann and Truman spoke for forty-five minutes. Weizmann had no new facts or arguments to bring to the meeting. But he knew how to approach someone in power. He was not the abrasive Abba Hillel Silver. Truman listened. No agreements emerged from the meeting. What did emerge was more elusive. Truman felt a bond with Weizmann. Maybe Eddie Jacobson's highly exaggerated claim of Weizmann being his hero was part of it. No doubt Weizmann himself was a great advocate for the Zionists. In any case, without specifics, a deep sense of connection developed between them.

That connection would be tested almost immediately.

Truman was pleased that evening. He took his wife, Bess, and his daughter, Margaret, to a concert. At intermission, he sneaked out to go to a war bonds rally a few blocks away and then returned for the end of the concert. The next morning, he told his staff that he was thinking of going on a cross-country tour during the summer.

All seemed well.

That morning at Lake Success, where the United Nations met, the American ambassador, Warren Austin, was preparing for a major policy statement. He was, in his mind at least, not knowingly going against Truman. Eleven days earlier onboard the presidential yacht, Truman had offered perfunctory approval for a State Department position paper. The department wanted the United States to go on record as accepting an international trusteeship to make sure that Jews and Arabs remained peaceful if the plans for partition could not be worked out adequately. Truman read it and saw the proposal as a vague possibility, not concrete. Indeed, he had explicitly told a friend on that same trip that he was still committed to partition. David Niles and Clark Clifford, who surely would have seen the political dangers of such a paper, were not with the president. Truman never saw what was about to happen coming because just a week earlier, he had sent an explicit order: "Nothing should be presented to the Security Council that could be interpreted as a recession on our part from the position we took in the General Assembly"—that is, a position in favor of partition.

The political bomb exploded on March 19. At the Security Council, Austin declared that the United States no longer believed that partition was a viable option for Palestine and the U.S. government favored an international trusteeship for the area. The American press was not kind either to the State Department or Truman for this breathtaking reversal. "Inept," "weak," "vacillating," and many other epithets found their way into the American press. One American commentator said, "I am ashamed of us."

The Arabs were, of course, elated. In the Land of Israel, David Ben-Gurion, feeling betrayed, was furious. He responded: "It is we who will determine the fate of Palestine. We cannot agree to any sort of trusteeship, permanent or temporary. The Jewish state exists because we defend it." Four days later, the Jewish Agency announced that it would establish a Jewish government in mid-May.

If possible, though, Truman felt more fury than Ben-Gurion.

Truman only found out what happened by reading the newspapers. It was Saturday, March 20, 1948. He looked at the papers and saw such headlines as "Reversal of United States Policy on Palestine." Other papers were less kind, comparing the United Nations to the failed League of Nations and darkly warning of the loss of American prestige.

Truman took to his diary to express his anger and his guilt about appearing to betray Weizmann, especially so soon after talking with him:

> The State Department has pulled the rug from under me today. Isn't that hell? I am now in a position of a liar and doublecrosser. I've never felt so low in my life. There are people on the third and fourth levels of the State Department who have always wanted to cut my throat. They've succeeded in doing it.

He wanted to call an immediate cabinet meeting, but cooler heads prevailed; any such meeting would have made the administration seem to be in disorder. Truman started by ordering Clark Clifford to determine exactly what had happened. Explanations were offered. Truman had read the position paper and didn't have any objections. There had been a clear lack of communication from the State Department.

It was determined that David Niles was needed. Despite heart problems, he returned to Washington.

By coincidence, that day Judge Sam Rosenman, an influential Jewish friend of Truman's, called, and the president asked his friend to contact Weizmann and tell him that Truman was being honest at their meeting just two days earlier. Truman wanted it made clear that the United States continued to support the partition of the land into a Jewish state and an Arab state. Furthermore, Truman wanted it stressed to Weizmann that the president did not know what was going to transpire at the United Nations. Rosenman did as he was asked.

Weizmann, of course, had been deeply upset by the original reports, and he was greatly relieved to get Rosenman's message. Weizmann also called Eddie Jacobson to tell him of the message.

Weizmann, unlike most American Zionists, understood the goal of the movement. The Zionists didn't much care about what the Americans said as long as America would recognize the Jewish nation when it was declared.

It was this goal to which Weizmann turned his full attention.

The Jewish leader had built such a bond with Truman that the American president had another message sent to the old and ailing Zionist: if a Jewish state were declared and the United Nations was struggling with a trusteeship, then Truman would recognize the Jewish state immediately. Truman, though, had one condition: Chaim Weizmann was the only leader with whom he would deal. Now it was Weizmann's turn to keep a confidence. He could tell no one about Harry Truman's secret promise of recognition.

Two men united by a moment in history learned to trust each other. Truman liked the manners of Weizmann. He respected Weizmann's history, his contributions to the World War I victory. It was, after all, a war in which Truman had fought. Between them, through agonizing weeks, they knew they could trust each other. And unbelievably, the trust worked.

The State Department wasn't so trusting of a president it thought put politics ahead of the national interest. It is unclear if anti-Semitism tainted the view of the State Department officials. Certainly, there were accusations of it. If the State Department believed that Truman was only pro-partition for political purposes, they weren't very good political analysts. If he was in it to garner votes for the upcoming 1948 election, Jews in New York would be a natural target. But Truman's presumptive opponent, Tom Dewey, was the sitting governor of New York State. In 1944, Dewey had been the Republican candidate for president and had given Franklin D. Roosevelt his closest race yet. It would be politically obtuse to think that Truman, even with a substantial Jewish vote, could win in New York. In fact, Truman lost New York. He also lost Pennsylvania and Illinois, two other states with large Jewish populations. Whatever any advisers might have suggested or opponents charged, it seems clear that Truman did just what he appeared to do: take his job as president seriously enough to make his decision based on the merits of the issue, not on political considerations.

Clark Clifford finished his examination, and the pro-partition forces in the White House set about their business. David Niles wanted to make sure that the reliable John H. Hilldring, who had been a general during the Second World War, was appointed special assistant to the secretary of state for Palestine affairs. The State Department bitterly opposed such an appointment. Weizmann, recognizing a friend when he saw one, telephoned Hilldring six times, trying to convince him to take the job. Hilldring ended up not accepting the job, but the very fact that the president wanted someone with his views had a profound effect on the State Department.

Still, the department did not easily surrender its views. It might be thought that the sides were obvious: American Jews on one side, the State Department on the other. But the reality was far more complex. Eventually, as Israel became a reality and as the horrors of the Holocaust became more widely known, most American Jews would become Zionists to some extent or another, especially after the Six-Day War of 1967. But in early 1948, there was still no Israel. The Holocaust's full dimensions were still slowly working their way through the conscience of the world. And American Jews were still divided about Zionism.

The State Department took advantage of this and approached Judah Magnes. Born in San Francisco, Magnes had been a pacifist during the First World War, a passionate advocate of a single binational state in Palestine, a very prominent Reform rabbi, and, crucially for the State Department's plotters, head of the famous Hebrew University of Jerusalem. Albert Einstein, one of the university's founders, had a particular dislike for Magnes and resigned from the university's Board of Governors when Magnes gained control of academic affairs. Einstein wrote:

> The bad thing about the business was that the good Felix Warburg thanks to his financial authority ensured that the incapable Magnes was made director of the Institute, a failed American rabbi, who, through his dilettantish enterprises had become uncomfortable to his family in America, who very much hoped to dispatch him honorably to some exotic place. This ambitious and weak person surrounded himself with other morally inferior men, who did not allow any decent person to succeed there. . . . These people managed to poison the atmosphere there totally and to keep the level of the institution low.

Despite Einstein's dramatic gesture, American Jews attached the name of Magnes to the illustrious educational institution he ran. Magnes arrived in New York on April 21, 1948, and four days later proclaimed that a Jewish state would not survive, that the Arabs would overrun it. As a Jew running a prominent university in Jerusalem, Magnes was in a position to be influential. His belief in Arab and Jewish cooperation, a view that in retrospect seems incredibly naive, was a view shared earlier by other prominent Jews, including Martin Buber. Had Magnes come to America a year earlier, his voice may have had a profound influence, but as it was much of American Jewish opinion about a Jewish state had begun to firm up because of the heady rush of events and the realization of the truth of the Holocaust. Magnes and the State Department were too late.

Even then, however, the road was not clear. The Zionists themselves were divided about whether to declare a state unilaterally when the British left, or delay, hoping for a U.N. effort to find a peaceful resolution with the Arabs. Abba Hillel Silver was adamantly opposed to any delay. Menachem Begin, the Irgun leader, said that if Ben-Gurion didn't declare a state, he would. But others in the Jewish Agency were more cautious. No one cherished the idea of fighting multiple Arab armies.

Even at this late hour, the State Department was not ready to surrender. Warren Austin was living in the Waldorf Astoria Hotel because of his role as U.N. ambassador. As it happened, Chaim Weizmann was living in the same hotel. Austin paid a visit on the old man, considered by everyone to be moderate in both temperament and views. But if Austin and his colleagues thought that Weizmann would see the wisdom in a delay of the declaration of a Jewish state, they were deeply disappointed. Weizmann, of course, knew what they didn't. He knew Harry Truman would recognize the new state independent of any influence from the State Department.

Weizmann's uncharacteristically strong endorsement of an immediate declaration also struck those in the Jewish Agency who were wavering as unusual. Chaim Weizmann was just not a vehement man, but at this moment on this question of whether or not to declare a Jewish state, Weizmann was unmoving in his determination to convince others of his view. This was, after all, Chaim Weizmann, Zionist icon. He was not to be easily dismissed.

Truman came under even more enormous pressure. At one meeting, George C. Marshall, secretary of state and widely considered an American hero, confronted the president about the plan to recognize an independent Jewish state. So strong were Marshall's arguments that at one point Truman jokingly said, "Well, General, it sounds to me as if even you might vote against me in November if I go ahead to recognize." Unlike Truman, Marshall didn't believe in joking around. Instead, he said, "Yes, Mr. President, if I were to vote at all, I might just do that."

On May 14, 1948, David Ben-Gurion stood in the Tel Aviv Museum. More than 350 people packed the room. Two large flags and a portrait of political Zionism's founder, Theodor Herzl, hung above Ben-Gurion's head.

Ben-Gurion was waiting until 4:00 p.m., time enough before the Jewish Sabbath began, to read the Israeli Declaration of Independence.

When the declaration finally arrived, Ben-Gurion picked up his walnut gavel. He pounded the gavel and began to read the declaration that, as of midnight on May 15, declared Jewish sovereignty in the Land of Israel for the first time in almost two thousand years.

By diplomatic rules, in order for the United States to recognize the new nation of Israel, someone representing that new state had to apply for recognition. Clark Clifford, unable to reach Niles, frantically searched for the right person to apply. After talking to various people, Clifford and David Ginsburg, a lawyer who served as the Jewish Agency's counsel, worked together to draft the request for America to recognize Israel. They gave the draft to Eliahu Epstein (later Eilat), then the Jewish Agency's representative in Washington. Epstein submitted the request. Only then did he call the Jewish Agency overseas and request permission to do so.

The request landed in Secretary Marshall's office. Epstein had been authorized to "express the hope that your government will recognize and will welcome Israel into the community of nations."

President Truman announced the U.S. recognition at 6:11 p.m. on May 14, just after midnight in Israel.

> This government has been informed that a Jewish state has been declared in Palestine, and recognition has been requested by the provisional government thereof.
>
> The United States recognizes the provisional government as the de facto authority of the new State of Israel.

After he did so, Truman spoke of Chaim Weizmann to an aide, saying, "The Old Doctor will believe me now." Truman then called David Niles and said, "Dave, I want you to know that I've just announced recognition. You're the first person I called because I knew how much this would mean to you."

Weizmann was in New York having tea with friends. His political aide rushed into the room. But Weizmann, of course, did not need to be told. The old Zionist said, "President Truman has recognized our state."

His shocked aide asked, "How could you know? You don't have a radio."

Weizmann replied, "I saw it in your face."

At ten that evening, the White House received a telegram. It was from Eddie Jacobson to Harry Truman: "Thanks and God bless you."

The next day, Abe Granoff, another Truman friend, wrote to the president in his name and Jacobson's.

> You know that Eddie Jacobson's and my confidence in you on Palestine never wavered. . . . We felt that you were doing everything possible for the Jewish people abroad. . . . We always recognized your anxiety to avoid bloodshed. . . . If Eddie and I and others shed a tear of gratitude, you above all can understand. So, also, will you understand if Chaim Weizmann's eyes were moist when he talked to Eddie a few minutes ago.

David Ben-Gurion had gone to sleep early on the evening of May 14. He more than anyone else knew that Israel's future was not certain. He had been warned that the Israelis had only a 50 percent chance of surviving the coming Arab attack. Ben-Gurion knew he needed some rest. Just after one o'clock in the morning, Ben-Gurion's planned rest came to an end. He received a telephone call informing him that the United States had officially recognized the new Jewish nation.

The chief of the Haganah burst into Ben-Gurion's bedroom against the furious objections of Ben-Gurion's wife, Paula. The chief wanted Ben-Gurion to make a radio broadcast aimed at the United States.

Ben-Gurion put a coat over his pajamas and went over to the broadcast studio. He knew he had to make the statement. He had barely begun when the studio was hit by bombs. "Listen," Ben-Gurion cried out to his audience, "those are the sounds of bombs falling on Tel Aviv."

Also in Tel Aviv, a little after midnight, Golda Meir, then still Golda Meyerson, was alone in her apartment when the telephone rang. Golda expected bad news, but as she picked up the phone, she heard the extraordinary news of American recognition. She later recalled, "It was like a miracle coming at a time of our greatest vulnerability on the eve of the invasion. I was filled with joy and relief. All Israel rejoiced and gave thanks."

There were celebrations all over the world. In America, people celebrated by dancing the hora in the streets. They waved tiny blue-and-white flags representing Israel. Shouts of "mazel tov" could be heard throughout the land.

Perhaps one of the most poignant moments came near Salzburg, Austria. U.S. Army chaplain Oscar M. Lifshutz was set to begin the Sabbath service for the Holocaust refugees at the Riedenberg displaced persons camp. Suddenly, a jeep approached. Colonel Long, a senior officer at army headquarters, arrived unannounced. Long approached Lifshutz. "Chaplain, I'm a Protestant, but I feel that I too have given a helping hand in bringing these children of Israel to freedom. I want to be able to tell my children how I once helped a people to find their home." The colonel made a gesture and two American MPs walked to the flagpole, lowered the flying American flag, folded it according to regulations, saluted, and handed the flag to the colonel. Long then marched to the leader of the inmates in the displaced persons camp and handed him the American flag, saying, "We want you to remember us."

The survivor, choked up and unable to speak, took the flag and signaled another inmate carrying a bundle under his arm. The bundle was a flag of Israel, homemade by the inmates. Two of the survivors raised the new flag on the flagpole. Together, the refugees and American soldiers sang "Hatikvah," the Israeli national anthem, and "America the Beautiful."

3

ORGANIZING FOR ACTION

During the daylight hours, Haim Slavin served as the director of the Land of Israel's most important power station, the Palestine Electric Company. Slavin, forty-four, was stocky, with blue eyes that focused on a person with unnerving concentration. He had sandy hair, a Slavic face, and a cantankerous nature. He, like Ben-Gurion, was a man who had seemingly taken a vow never to smile.

The job at the power station was a good one for an ordinary man with an extraordinary grasp of engineering, physics, and chemistry. But Slavin was far from ordinary. After his day job ended, Slavin turned to his passion. He was the Haganah's specialist in secretly producing arms to use in a future fight against the Arabs.

As an arms expert, Slavin constantly scanned the news looking for untapped opportunities and ideas. And so it was that he sat at a sidewalk café in Tel Aviv one evening in the early summer of 1945. He was reading the newspaper, characteristically quickly looking over its contents for any useful material. Suddenly, he came across a brief story with a Washington, DC, dateline. The story was about seven hundred thousand machine tools, most of them new or nearly new, that would over the upcoming months be converted into scrap metal.

The birth of ideas comes at unplanned moments in odd ways. Up until reading the story, Slavin, like Ben-Gurion, like the Haganah, like everyone associated with the Land of Israel's efforts to defend the

Yishuv—the Jewish community in the land—had a simple understanding of their defense needs and the task that stood in front of them. Their job was to acquire weapons by purchasing them. That was why they needed money and why Ben-Gurion had spoken to the Sonneborn Institute.

But in an instant, Slavin, the argumentative and ill-tempered but brilliant chemist, had another vision. He had already dreamed a dream that seemed impossible, that, indeed, was mocked when he had first presented it.

He wanted the *Yishuv* not just to buy weapons but also to manufacture its own. And now it was possible, he claimed; now the idea had jumped from his mind to reality. The raw material he needed to build those weapons was right there in the United States.

Slavin ran home to his two-room apartment and sent a letter to Ben-Gurion outlining his plan. He noted that history had offered the Jews a unique opportunity. The chance to get such machinery would not happen again. What was needed, Slavin suggested, was to go to America, get the materials, smuggle them past the British into the Land of Israel, and use them as the basis of a new armaments industry.

But Slavin knew he needed proof that what he wanted to do was possible, that weapons could be manufactured by the Jews themselves. And so, in his own kitchen, he began to build hand grenades and TNT detonators.

Ben-Gurion was impressed, and in September 1945, the Jewish leader sent Slavin to the United States. His mission was to buy that necessary machinery at the war surplus sales then being held throughout the United States. He was then to get everything to Palestine. Slavin received a list of contacts, especially Rudolf Sonneborn and Henry Montor, but the list was accompanied by Ben-Gurion's stern warning to stay far away from American Zionist leaders. This must have confused Slavin. After all, if they were Zionists, wouldn't they want to help build Zion? He didn't grasp the intricacies of American Jews' self-perceptions and fear of the accusation of dual loyalty. American Jews generally had very different perceptions of Jewish life in Palestine than did the Jews who lived there. American Jews weren't surrounded by enemy nations. They lived in a prosperous nation, but one that didn't have a Jewish identity.

Slavin faced many challenges as he went to New York. His English was poor. Knowing he needed to improve it, he took with him a 1924 edition of the Sherlock Holmes stories, which he diligently read with the aid of a dictionary.

It was a ninety-hour flight from Tel Aviv to New York. Slavin telephoned Montor the morning following his arrival. Montor amazingly arranged for him to move into the Hotel Commodore near Grand Central Station. The hotel was then crowded with postwar guests competing for rooms. Rudolf Sonneborn took Slavin to an expensive restaurant and fed him a hearty lunch. He had no idea how to use the fancy utensils and told Sonneborn to begin eating and Slavin would observe and follow.

After a failed lead in Chicago, Slavin returned to New York looking for help. He was discouraged, frustrated by his speech, and without the necessary contacts. So he disobeyed Ben-Gurion's orders to stay away from people who had come from the Land of Israel. Slavin called a friend, grateful to converse in Hebrew. The man knew of Slavin's secret work in munitions and sent Slavin to a contact at a youth organization. There Slavin repeated his need to find someone as an assistant. The contact listened. As it turned out, he told Slavin, he had recently been in contact with a friend from California, a young Jewish engineer who needed a job. Best of all, he was an American citizen and could purchase the surplus military equipment.

Phil Alper had been born in Syracuse, New York, in 1924. He and his parents moved to Los Angeles in the 1930s. He graduated from Berkeley in 1945. He was twenty-one, good-looking, and adventurous. The thought of taking a typical job as a new mechanical engineer horrified him. His heart murmur had kept him out of the Second World War, and that, combined with the fact that his two older brothers had served, bothered him. He was patriotic, but he was also a young man who craved excitement. He considered moving to Alaska to start anew.

Instead, in September 1945 Alper hitchhiked across the country to New York City. Once he arrived, Alper moved in with an uncle. He checked the classified ads. He also called an old friend who had once been members with him in a Zionist youth group. The friend, the man who had been in contact with Haim Slavin, said, "Phil, I have a job for you." Suspicious, Alper said he wasn't interested in Zionist work, only in engineering. The friend assured him it was an engineering job, but he added, "It has something to do with Palestine. That's all I can tell you."

Deciding to take a chance, the next day Alper went with his friend to the Hotel Commodore. The two took the elevator up to the twelfth floor.

Haim Slavin opened the door.

Alper entered the tiny room and looked at the small desk, the chair, the window, and the bed.

Slavin bowed ever so slightly, put out his hand, and introduced himself.

Alper sat down in the chair and waited. Left alone with the stocky stranger after his friend left, Alper surely must have wondered how the man in front of him could offer him a job.

Slavin, in his hesitant and broken English, asked Alper to speak about his experience. Impressed, Slavin described himself as someone who had left Russia in 1924 bound for Palestine, how in 1929 he had been caught up in the Arab riots, noting that the seven hundred Jews he was with were surrounded and the only weapons they had to defend themselves were six hand grenades. Slavin explained that he had sent some men to Haifa in search of pipe fittings and explosives and then had the men stuff two-inch pipe sections with dynamite and a fuse that lasted four seconds. In that way, he made a few hundred homemade grenades. He noted dryly that after the riots he knew "we should start to do something more serious to protect ourselves." That was when he began work for the Haganah secretly making weapons. Slavin went on, explaining his efforts during the Second World War, discussing how weapons had to be made despite British efforts to prevent the Jews from doing so.

And then Slavin got to the point. He told Alper the truth: Slavin was in the United States to acquire the machinery necessary to set up an arms industry for the Jews in Palestine. After getting the machinery, it all then had to be shipped overseas. Slavin said that because of his poor English, his lack of knowledge about American life and customs, and his sheer foreignness, he himself could not go around getting the information necessary to accomplish this job. That was what he wanted Alper to do.

Alper, quietly doubting the Jews could make weapons while the British controlled the country, had one major concern. "Will this be against American law?"

Slavin wanted to explain the idea of a higher morality, that after the Holocaust smuggling weapons and materials to protect Jews made questions of civil law morally trivial. Slavin thought that America, as a beacon of hope and democracy for all the world, would understand this. But Slavin also knew the realities of political life. He spoke as well as he could. "You cannot live without a spirit in the law. That is why you go to a judge and not to a machine that says yes or no automatically." Slavin struggled to continue. He said that everyone in America with "the picture of the night that is coming to Palestine and the dark forces coming around us will understand."

Alper put aside his desire to ask for a few days to consider the proposal when he saw Slavin's anxiety-ridden face.

"All right," Alper said, "I'll start Monday."

Slavin, armed with chutzpah and directness, said, "What's the matter with tomorrow?"

The next morning, the two first agreed on a weekly salary of thirty-five dollars. Alper, thinking he would be participating in a heady tale of adventure, at first wound up in the New York Public Library looking for articles in technical journals about arms manufacturing. As he compiled his lists, careful to avoid listing the provocative-sounding titles of the articles, Alper visited various magazine shops with back issues as their specialty. H. W. Wilson Company in the Bronx was the most impressive location. Alper took the magazines back to Slavin's small room, and the two men spent hours together poring through the magazines. Alper would read an article and explain it to Slavin, who in turn made some notes. Alper clipped the articles pertinent to the acquisition of the sorts of arms and materials Slavin wanted. Slowly, they began to organize the articles and illustrations, pasting them in order on loose-leaf pages and then putting the pages into a scrapbook. They were slowly assembling an arms manual.

Their hushed conversations continued at lunches at an automat. Slavin began to focus on a particular project. What the Jews in Palestine needed most was a gun, a weapon they could learn to use easily, a weapon available to protect their homes from the terrorists, a weapon small enough to hide easily but powerful enough to be a real force in any fight.

It was Rudolf Sonneborn who, once again, came to the rescue. Sonneborn introduced Slavin to Harry Levine, a remarried widower in his late forties. Levine, a millionaire who owned a plastics manufacturing company in Leominster, Massachusetts, had been in the arms business during the Second World War as an owner of the New York Safe and Lock Company, which had made parts for a Swiss gun. His personal life made Levine seem too old and settled to recruit for a clandestine operation, but he turned out to be an incredible asset. Levine was willing to make contact with American arms manufacturers throughout the United States. He served as the front man for Machinery Processing and Supply, a company Slavin established.

Slavin told Levine about his dream for "the Gun." In October 1945, a friend of Levine told him about another friend, a non-Jewish Swedish engineer named Carl Ekdahl, who might be interested in developing the weapon. (This friend of Levine's and Ekdahl's is unknown, though it is possible that it was David Dardick, a Russian-born Jewish engineer and inventor.)

Ekdahl had been born in Sweden and in 1910, at age eighteen, he emigrated to the United States. During World War I, he found work as a gunsmith. He crucially helped develop the Johnson light machine gun, known for being both simple and versatile. A heart attack in 1942

ORGANIZING FOR ACTION

forced him to quit work. The inactivity irked him because he had been an active hunter and fisherman, a man who enjoyed participating in a rousing Swedish song, a robust man who enjoyed good food and a tasty drink. He wanted to get back to being a gunsmith but realized the difficulty of doing so.

It was then that Harry Levine called him, mentioned their mutual friend, and talked carefully about small matters. Finally, Levine began his pitch. Was Ekdahl interested, Levine wanted to know, in designing another machine gun, one similar to the Johnson? The design was needed for a small research project that Levine was considering.

Ekdahl and Levine agreed to meet the next day at the Hotel Commodore. Levine wanted him to meet an associate.

Haim Slavin hid his magazines in a closet and sent Phil Alper out while he met with Ekdahl. The man Slavin needed walked into the room carrying a canvas case, one with a clear outline marking its contents. Ekdahl was walking around with a machine gun. Slavin nearly fainted because in his country, such an action was unthinkably dangerous, an illegal act, a guaranteed prison sentence by the British.

Ekdahl handed over his Johnson light machine gun to Slavin and carefully pointed out the gun's qualities. While it was lighter than virtually any other machine gun, it nevertheless fired rifle cartridges that were full-sized. It was, that is, a weapon meant for a fight. Ekdahl showed Slavin how to flip a switch and transform the weapon into a semiautomatic useful for snipers. Slavin was very happy.

Ekdahl proposed to Slavin that the gun be redesigned to include the Johnson's up-to-date features. Slavin slipped out of his personality and smiled. Ekdahl invited Slavin to his home in Providence, and Slavin accepted.

Slavin was ill when he arrived at the Ekdahl home, but Hilda Ekdahl was ready. She had him lie down in bed and fed him tea and aspirin. Slavin was profoundly moved by this non-Jewish couple who took care of him. He and Ekdahl then spent several days talking about the much-needed gun. Slavin tried to sit up in his bed, and the Swedish gunsmith stayed in a chair beside him.

Slavin was nervous. He needed Ekdahl to design the gun and its machinery. It was time to gamble. Slavin said he was a Jew from the Land of Israel and that his people needed weapons to defend themselves. Ekdahl said he was sympathetic to the idea of a Jewish nation. He said he would help the Jews be able to defend themselves.

A deal was worked out. Ekdahl would get $17,000 for his efforts, which he estimated would take six months.

Slavin's nightmare came about after several months of work. Ekdahl came to visit him in New York with a dilemma. A group of Egyptians had approached Ekdahl with a proposition. They also wanted him to build a gun. Only they offered $100,000 for the job. Ekdahl, with little money, a tiny pension, and a large family, was deeply troubled. Slavin said, "You owe nothing to the Jewish people. I free you from the contract."

Ekdahl's conscience persisted in bothering him, and he asked Slavin to come with him and discuss it with his wife. Once there, Ekdahl explained his offer.

"Carl," she asked, "You have a contract with this man?"

Ekdahl said he did.

"Is this man fulfilling his obligations?"

"Of course."

"Well then," Hilda Ekdahl concluded in her almost musical Swedish accent, "there's nothing to talk about. Just get on with the job."

It is not clear why, but Slavin settled on Toronto, Canada, as the site for building "the Gun." Perhaps the reason was that Samuel J. Zacks, an ardent Zionist financier who was the only Canadian to attend the meeting at Rudolf Sonneborn's apartment, was from Toronto and could help with organizing the effort. Zacks got Norman Grant, who had managed York Arsenals in Toronto during World War II, to help.

Workspace was found above a showroom for luxury cars. The separate entrance and the helpful racket from cars downstairs was perfect. Industrial Research Labs was almost in business, but references were needed. Once again, Harry Levine came to the rescue by cosigning the lease.

Grant proved to be crucial because his war work made him familiar with people who had the greatest skills. Grant hired Max Brown, and together they ordered the precision tools necessary. In all, the Gun was going to require fifteen hundred steps.

As work continued on the Gun, Slavin had much other work to do. First, he realized he needed a safer and much larger location and found it in a five-room apartment at 512 West 112th Street in New York. Alper moved into an apartment two doors away, and the men began working seven days a week, routinely putting in eighteen-hour days.

Slavin and Alper's work expanded because of the formation of the War Assets Administration. This government agency was established to sell surplus war supplies and plants. It was like a giant sale with all sorts of goods available at a one-time bargain price.

Alper and Slavin got on all the mailing lists they could that provided information about the surplus goods. When they found an interesting potential purchase, Alper, the American who could do the actual buying, went to examine the goods. It was in Bridgeport, Connecticut, that Alper made his first big purchase: six tons of machinery. This was necessary to produce ammunition for the Gun.

After trouble at their warehouse, Slavin realized that a new location, one safe from prying eyes, was needed. They eventually found one in the Bronx. In New Bedford, Massachusetts, Alper put in a high bid and won six trailer-loads of machinery. The two men then took a trip through the Midwest. They bought a 1936 Chevrolet to save money on trains and buses.

The warehouse was gradually being filled with a variety of goods.

Slavin and Alper had organized the effort, done the research, and were busy buying all the surplus materials. None of that was illegal. But the materials sitting in a warehouse in New York were of no use to the Jews in the Land of Israel. Those goods had to be shipped out of the United States and smuggled into Palestine. That was illegal at both ends.

A separate person was needed for that task.

Elie Schalit was twenty-two, blond, with an enormous gift for language. He spoke with Phil Alper and sounded British. His Hebrew was more fluent than Slavin's. He was a sabra, born in the Land of Israel. He had begun working for the Haganah while still in high school, but his extraordinary ability to speak with people, his boldness, his knowledge of military tactics, his travels and studies around the world, had marked him out. He was the man for Slavin.

Schalit's smooth, debonair approach was desperately needed. He couldn't be caught. The State Department was supposed to give permission for all arms shipments abroad. Schalit, unlike Alper and anyone else who shopped for materials, was explicitly violating American laws. If he was discovered, the entire operation was in danger, and those who helped him faced the possibility of legal action. If Schalit's shipments were captured in Palestine, those who helped faced British justice. That meant terms in jail.

Schalit's job was complex. Figuring out how to pack and ship the machinery was the easy part of the job. It was Schalit's way with people, his undeniable ability to talk his way out of any situation, to talk to people in such a way that he could conduct a master class in being a con man that proved his most vital strength. He needed to obtain the documents that were needed for shipping and export licenses. He had to deal with the port authorities in the United States and in the Land of Israel. He had to make sure that the customs inspectors in both places didn't look too carefully at what was being sent. Some of the materials could be legitimately shipped, but for the materials used for making weapons, their actual purpose had to be carefully camouflaged. A lathe might be used for a weapon, to be sure. But it also could be used to make a shovel.

Schalit focused on the materials that required a disguise. The complex process began by dismantling the materials. Each part was carefully marked with a number. The number and part were recorded on a card. There were eventually seventy thousand separate parts listed on those cards. A drawing was made describing how the particular machine was to be reassembled. The parts, now separated, were put randomly among other machine parts so that their end use could not be identified. Alper discovered large crates, too unwieldy for careful inspection, and these were used for shipping.

Schalit roamed the docks, meeting workers, discovering what kind of power and money were needed and where in order to get the work done. He made sure to have someone at the docks for each shipment made. He wanted to be sure of success.

Just as the process was put into place, however, there was a disruption. In the fall of 1946, Haim Slavin received orders. He was to return to Palestine, where the one hundred thousand British troops had made arms manufacturing an increasingly precarious enterprise. Slavin's unique skills, so useful in New York, were now required more urgently in Palestine.

Slavin told his assistants that they could contact someone else, Jacob Dostrovsky, later known as Yaakov Dori, who became the Israel Defense Forces' first chief of staff. Dostrovsky had become head of the American Haganah delegation in January 1946.

Alper continued to communicate with Slavin, moved into the apartment, and began to take over more tasks. It was Alper who received word that two prototypes of the Gun were ready to be transported for testing from Toronto to Carl Ekdahl's Vermont farm.

It was a Monday afternoon, February 24, 1947. Carl Ekdahl, Norman Grant, and Max Brown, affectionately known as Maxie, piled into Ekdahl's 1942 Mercury and headed for the Whirlpool Bridge to cross the border into the United States. Two of the six prototypes of the Gun were in the trunk, carefully separated into stock, barrel, and firing mechanisms. There were a hundred rounds of .303 ammunition, which had been much easier to purchase in Canada than in the United States. They stopped in Hamilton, Ontario, to get another car for the crossing, dividing the weapons between the two cars. A business friend who provided the car also arranged for one of his employees, a man named Andrew Noseworthy who knew nothing about the weapons, to drive Max Brown to Buffalo, New York. Some of the material was put under the front seat of the second car, and Brown had to keep pushing it back with his foot.

The two cars went on their journey, separated by only a few other cars. Ekdahl and Grant crossed first. They parked on a highway waiting for Brown.

Brown had arrived at the crossing. A guard came over to ask him how long he was going to spend in the United States. Three days, Brown had responded, in order to visit a girlfriend. The guard then went over to Noseworthy, who, despite instructions about what he was to say, simply told the truth, that he was driving the passenger to Buffalo and would immediately return. The guard had Brown step out of the car and began to search it. He quickly discovered the weapons materials.

Meanwhile, Ekdahl and Grant were growing increasingly worried about Brown's absence. They fortified themselves against the winter cold with whisky. Then they went to a café. Still no Brown.

After waiting an hour, the two decided to go back to the bridge. It was there they discovered that the police had Brown and Noseworthy in custody. Ekdahl and Grant went to the Statler Hotel in Buffalo, where Grant called Phil Alper. This should have been a time to panic, but Alper stayed calm. He told Grant to stay there, that both Alper and Dostrovsky would travel to Buffalo.

A "fixer" was needed. Dostrovsky called Harry Levine, who was on vacation in Florida. Levine told his wife that their vacation was over, that he was needed. His wife said she would travel with him.

Maxie Brown was put in the Erie County jail in Buffalo. For three days, he was questioned by a variety of men, two from the Federal Bureau of Investigation (FBI) and two from the Royal Canadian Mounted Police. They threatened to put him in a cell with "Daisy," a powerful homosexual. But Brown, answering their questions with simple words as though he didn't know much, held out. He refused even to make a phone call. He knew that he needed to give Alper and the others time to escape.

In fact, Alper and Dostrovsky were extremely worried that Harry Levine's name would be discovered, because if the FBI investigated him, all the documents he signed would emerge and the entire effort in America would be endangered.

They formulated a plan. Toronto was sacrificed; the office there was to be the headquarters of the gun plot. Grant, arrested after his return to Canada, pleaded guilty and paid his fine. The police could not prove that he worked for Palestine. Grant received the machinery back once he paid the fine.

Maxie Brown's trial was held in Rochester, New York, in May. Brown's attorney and Judge Harold Burke briefly conferred. Burke, clearly sympathetic to the Zionist cause or at least, as an Irishman, clearly unsympathetic to the British, fined Brown one hundred dollars and told him to stay out of the United States for one year.

Levine was still worried. He knew how efficient the FBI was under J. Edgar Hoover. Surely they hadn't been fooled by Brown's naive act. After some phone calls had been made, Levine, Dostrovsky, and another man flew down to Washington, DC, to meet with Robert Nathan, an economist and staunch Zionist. More important, Nathan was friends with Hoover.

The FBI was in charge of enforcing the embargo on arms shipments to the Land of Israel. But the shrewd and powerful Hoover was friends with many people supportive of the Zionist cause and chose not to see all that happened.

Nathan and Hoover spoke quietly in a meeting in Hoover's car. Nathan explained the whole truth, that the machinery was being smuggled to the Jews in Palestine. Nathan noted with complete accuracy that if the operation was exposed, some important people and organizations might be hurt by the publicity. Hoover assessed the situation. He asked if the weapons that would be made were meant for use in the United States. Nathan assured him that they were not. Hoover pressed. Would they be used against the United States? Again, Nathan said they wouldn't. At that point, Hoover ended the conversation without a promise, but he clearly showed his sympathy. The Royal Canadian

Mounted Police had requested that the FBI undertake an investigation of the incident at the border in order to track down those involved, but if there was any real investigation, it did not lead to any arrests. Harry Levine and the effort to smuggle weapons were safe.

However safe the weapons were, though, they still needed to be shipped to Palestine. The intrepid Elie Schalit was put in charge of the problem. The special dies, the tools that were used to cut, shape, or stamp a material or object, were the particular problem, since an alert customs agent could recognize their true purpose. Schalit decided to scatter all the materials among his regular shipments.

His first problem was getting all the material to New York from Canada. Schalit showed up in Toronto with his twin sister. They carried fancy new luggage with them and stayed at the Prince Edward Hotel. It was there that they received several packages, including one with materials for the Gun. A clothing manufacturer from Toronto was drafted to help. He invited the Schalits on his yacht for a cruise. Several other people were invited so that the luggage on the dock that Schalit brought along with his special cargo looked like a wealthy person's suitcases for a fancy cruise. The yacht, loaded with fishing gear and wine, crossed Lake Ontario and reached Rochester. There a customs inspector looked at the people on the yacht, who held up their glasses of wine and waved at him. He waved back and let them enter. Schalit, his sister, and his special luggage got off the yacht and went to a car waiting to take them to New York, where a year later than the originally scheduled date, he sent the parts for the Gun to his homeland.

Jacob Dostrovsky, meanwhile, went back to Hotel Fourteen to continue other efforts. The attempt to get all sorts of materials from the United States involved a variety of missions. For the sake of security, people involved in each of these efforts didn't know anyone involved in efforts other than their own. There were inevitably meetings among various participants, but insofar as it was possible, the Haganah tried to maintain a need-to-know basis for every project such as the Gun.

But someone had to be in charge. Someone had to know every project. Jacob Dostrovsky was that man, and Hotel Fourteen was his headquarters.

Dostrovsky was deceptive. He was short and balding. His tan, the freckles, his horn-rimmed glasses, his gentleness despite a rugged appearance, and his friendly manner were perfect for American work. Underneath, though, Dostrovsky was tough. At age six, he had lived through a pogrom in Odessa. He fought in the Jewish Legion during World War I. After the war, he developed a new concept: Jewish communities in which the inhabitants learned how to be farmers and fighters. This dual concept became the model for the way Jews learned to defend themselves from attacks by Arabs during the 1920s in Palestine.

His new assignment in America was perfect for him. And he found the perfect headquarters.

Hotel Fourteen, named after its address, was owned by Ruby Barnett and his wife, Fannie. They had purchased the hotel in 1944. It was in 1945 that Fannie received a request. Was there a room available for a Jew from the Land of Israel? Fannie, a longtime Zionist, had been Chaim Weizmann's secretary when he came to the United States during World War II. She had also worked for the Jewish Agency for Palestine, and in 1945 they had asked her to return to help Reuven Zaslani (later known as Shiloah), the man David Ben-Gurion had sent ahead to look for people in the Jewish establishment to help him prior to realizing that he had to bypass the mainstream Jewish community, the conclusion that eventually led him to Rudolf Sonneborn. It was Fannie who had typed all the letters to the American Jewish leaders.

Hotel Fourteen had a split personality. There were wealthy people who lived there, transients who needed a room for the night, those filled with Zionist intrigue, and people looking for a good time.

The latter group came at night to the basement of Hotel Fourteen. The Copacabana was a night club in that basement. The place had tropical decor and barely clad women in a chorus line, with imitation pieces of fruit placed strategically across key parts of their bodies. That chorus line contributed to the Copa's great success, along with a string of popular performers that included Lena Horne and Dean Martin and his partner Jerry Lewis.

Once Dostrovsky moved into his room, Fannie went to work for him, dutifully typing letters. They worked well together.

Dostrovsky considered the obstacles he faced. He worked with Slavin to identify what was needed. For example, Dostrovsky knew that there were many Jewish communities in the Land of Israel that were isolated. They had no means to communicate with each other, share information, and, perhaps most crucially, organize communal defense. The British would go into these communities in search of illegal arms and seize any they found. Essentially, the British served the Arab attackers, because once the British took the weapons, the Jews were defenseless, and so the Arabs would soon follow the British visits with attacks. The isolated communities needed to know if the British were on the way.

A secret radio network was needed. Searching among his contacts, Dostrovsky came across Dan Fliderblum, a Yonkers electronics engineer who was so young he had not even been eligible to fight in the Second World War and then deferred because he turned out to be so critical as he trained people at New York University for their assignment with the U.S. Army Signal Corps. Fliderblum's constant appearance of being sleepy was deceptive; he was bright and alert and well connected. He knew the brilliant men who had served in the signal corps.

Now all of twenty-one, Fliderblum began his work. These young men Fliderblum was training built what appeared to be a radio. Its mahogany case was attractive. It worked well. But the crystal had been altered. It wasn't built to receive but to transmit.

Fliderblum, working in the way Phil Alper had, went around doing the purchasing. He was in constant search for radio equipment that could be used and found some great bargains, for which he needed a lot of money.

He got the money from Dostrovsky in the offices of Louis Rocker. When Dostrovsky needed money for his purchases, he and Fannie took

ORGANIZING FOR ACTION

the IRT Lexington Avenue subway to Broad Street, where they went into the offices of Louis Rocker. Rocker was, in effect, the Haganah's underground banker. Fannie would pack her pocketbook with piles of Rocker's money and she and Dostrovsky were set to make purchases.

The big money that went through this underground bank, which funded all the underground operations, could not have been obtained without the help of the man at the center of the underground financial enterprise—Rudolf Sonneborn.

Sonneborn was a patient and careful man. Following the initial meeting at his apartment, he began contacting potential supporters, explaining the need for money and secrecy, and waited for instructions. Sonneborn always spoke of other matters first, careful about approaching as touchy a subject as arms for the Jews in the Land of Israel. He also began to expand his network, meeting with those who had been at the apartment and getting them to hold meetings of their own, slowly and carefully building his team.

When the Jews from Palestine needed money, they most frequently met with Sonneborn, who channeled them to the proper supporter.

It was not long after Jacob Dostrovsky's arrival that, as the master organizer, he saw a need to get the Sonneborn Institute into action. Ben-Gurion was coming back to the United States for another visit, and so the official institute work could begin.

Ben-Gurion arrived on July 7. It was then that he asked Rudolf Sonneborn to activate his informal group.

Sonneborn initially held a planning meeting in his apartment, and then in late July 1946, the first meeting of the Sonneborn Institute was held at the Hotel Astor. The six men at the meeting listened as Jacob Dostrovsky described the situation in which the Jews of Palestine found themselves.

On June 29, following the confiscation of arms at a Haganah underground storeroom near Haifa, the British had invaded the offices of the Jewish Agency. All the leaders had been arrested, except for Ben-Gurion, who was in Paris. That was why he had flown to New York. The situation was desperate.

The Haganah reorganized in New York into four branches. They needed arms, personnel, ships, and positive public opinion. Hotel Fourteen became the center for all their operations. The hotel became affectionately known as Kibbutz 14. The Jewish Agency set up an office nearby, at 16 East Sixty-Sixth Street.

Sonneborn began a formal arrangement. Every Thursday afternoon the group would meet in the El Patio Room, a private dining area on the second mezzanine at the Hotel McAlpin. Perhaps if these weren't Jewish business leaders, Sonneborn would have met at a golf club. But Jewish business leaders, he knew, could find time for lunch and could accomplish a lot at luncheon meetings. Starting at 12:30 p.m., the meetings finished with Sonneborn's characteristic precision exactly at 2:00 p.m. Sonneborn developed a set routine. He began each meeting with the same comments:

> I want to stress, as we always do at these meetings, that all of you here are either close collaborators or friends of our colleagues who have vouched for you. In the course of our discussions we expose certain activities. I know you will understand the necessity of extreme discretion in disclosing what you hear. Much of what we say will be useful in your task of helping us reach the public, but you must be guarded in how you disclose any information obtained here.

Perhaps there was some emotional comfort in the food, usually simply a buffet, or in the urgency and secrecy of the meeting or in the male company of each lunch. The meetings were in some way meant to match a Haganah need with a particular individual who could meet that need. There were some in attendance who could not accept a particular assigned request. It was then Sonneborn's duty to work the phones until he found someone who could finish the task. For example, Charles J. Rosenblum, who headed a finance company in Pittsburgh, was given the task to purchase eighty tons of steel and to spend $10,000 in acquiring walkie-talkies.

Sonneborn was able to identify various industry groups in the United States. He wanted a representative for each of those groups. Additionally, the supporters held local meetings to raise money. On October 17, 1946, Sonneborn's meeting led to an agreement to raise $100,000 a week until the end of the year, for a total of $1 million. Although that was a great deal of money in 1946, it still wasn't enough to meet the Haganah's enormous needs. Sonneborn called on everyone to hold meetings. By April 17, 1947, the institute had raised over half a million additional dollars.

There were frequent guests at these luncheons. For example, just in 1948 some of the guests included Golda Meir; Abba Eban; Teddy Kollek, later the famous mayor of Jerusalem; Moshe Shertok of the Jewish Agency; writers; and representatives of the Haganah. These people provided information but also, more importantly, inspiration. Those in attendance felt, quite correctly, that they were important, that they were making significant contributions, that they were profoundly affecting Jewish history.

Adolf Robison's father had visited Palestine with Sonneborn. That trip had cemented a permanent relationship. The son lived in New Jersey and worked as a textile converter. Robison's incredible mind for figures, his memory (he seemed to recall every shipping route), and his ability to recall the names of everyone he met were invaluable to the work of the institute. He soon became Sonneborn's assistant at the meetings and the liaison between the institute and the Haganah.

Sonneborn formed a subsidiary group meant to be a public face for the mainstream Jewish defense organization, as opposed to the more radical groups such as the Irgun or the Lehi (also called, derisively, the Stern Gang). The institute created Americans for Haganah and then opened an office.

Just as Slavin had been recalled, so too was Dostrovsky, who was needed in Palestine. In June 1947, Shlomo Rabinovich (later Shamir) replaced Dostrovsky. It was a huge adjustment for everyone in New York. Dostrovsky was professorial, thoughtful, patient, and friendly. Rabinovich was distant, wary of everyone and everything. Leonard Slater, in his groundbreaking book *The Pledge*, perfectly captured Rabinovich: "He was a man who looked every gift horse in the mouth to see if its teeth had been wired for sound by the British secret service." Starting out at the age of fifteen as a runner for the Haganah, Rabinovich fought Syrian snipers and served in the British army during World War II. He claimed to have been shot at forty-two times at a distance of under twenty-five yards.

Rabinovich was a shrewd observer of people and talent. He began attending meetings of the Sonneborn Institute and in the summer of 1947 approached one of the men in attendance. Nahum Bernstein was an attorney in New York.

During World War II, Bernstein, already a lawyer, served with the Office of Strategic Services (OSS; the predecessor to the Central Intelligence Agency). Bernstein trained agents to go overseas and infiltrate enemy territory.

After the war, Bernstein became the Jewish Agency's New York attorney, in charge of the $750,000 in funds the agency held.

As a lawyer, Bernstein set up various companies to aid Schalit in exporting arms. He also set up Materials for Palestine and various other organizations, all of which contributed.

Rabinovich had seen Bernstein, good-looking, self-assured, friendly, and obviously highly trained and capable, and decided to ask for a crucial favor. Given Bernstein's background, the favor made sense. Rabinovich wanted nothing less than for Bernstein to set up a secret school in Manhattan to train Jews from the Land of Israel in intelligence work, to be conducted in their homeland. It was an audacious proposal, made necessary because the British prevented any training in Palestine itself. There were no adequate instructors, and possession of even a single weapon carried a death penalty.

Searching for the right space, Bernstein settled on the National Council of Young Israel on West Sixteenth Street. There were regular evening classes for adults held at the Orthodox institution, and Bernstein intended to include his classes among them. Bernstein concluded that a course in codes and ciphers was the most crucial. He tried to recruit a Jewish leader in the field; the response was negative. Finally, Bernstein turned to an OSS acquaintance, an Episcopalian from Schenectady in upstate New York. The man, Geoffrey Mott-Smith, truly got into the spirit of the attempt to hide the school's true calling. Bernstein once showed up to find Mott-Smith wearing a yarmulke and swaying back and forth as Orthodox Jews did when studying. But in this case, it was cryptography, not the Talmud, under discussion.

Meanwhile, Meyer Birnbaum, who had been a captain in the army, was in a nearby classroom illustrating the finer points of using one's thumbs, piano wire, and knives to kill someone in close combat. Another teacher provided lessons in demolition techniques.

As good as the classes were, Bernstein was not going to limit training to classroom instruction. Once the students had completed classroom training, Bernstein took them to some farms in upstate New York where the students worked with explosives.

The course lasted for six weeks and had its own final examination, a technique Bernstein had learned from the rigorous training given to OSS agents. Each student had a target objective, access to a printing press for false documentation, and a week to accomplish the mission. After the week, each graduate filed a report, and the best one was read at graduation. Bernstein recalled one particular report. An agent had made his way into the Jewish Agency and discovered that a Mr. Rabinovich was in fact a Haganah agent in New York for a special mission. As it happened, Rabinovich was sitting in the room. He jumped up and sarcastically congratulated the man, and he knew his security needed an immediate fix.

But everyone was proud. It didn't take long for the school to "graduate" fifty or sixty young men, who became nicknamed the Shoo-Shoo boys, a term adapted from the Hebrew slang for a secret agent.

Meanwhile, weapons continued to be collected. People from all over the country sought to provide souvenir weapons. For example, there was once a call from a Catholic funeral parlor on Mulberry Street in Little Italy. When a representative got there, one of the people at the parlor opened a casket and, without uttering a word, handed over several pistols for use by the Jews fighting for independence. On another occasion, a pregnant woman entered the office of a member of the institute. She reached beneath her skirt and pulled out eight pistols. There were stories like these from all over the country. People of all religions were ready to help.

And yet with all the small weapons, with all the millions of dollars collected by the Sonneborn Institute, and with all the fighters trained, David Ben-Gurion remained deeply anxious. He assumed that an array of Arab armies would be united against the small number of Jews. He knew some of these armies, especially in Jordan, were very well trained. And he knew that these armies would have all the latest equipment.

In contrast, the Jewish fighters from the Haganah had never been able to obtain certain kinds of weapons such as tanks, aircraft, and artillery. Without these, Ben-Gurion feared, the Jews would have a very short-lived national revival. Ben-Gurion was not the type to spend his hours in agony. He made a decision.

He decided to call Yehuda Arazi.

Arazi, code-named Alon, was a living legend. Part of his fame came from the fact that in 1943, Arazi and a partner had stolen five thousand rifles from the British for use by the Haganah. Arazi immediately went into hiding for two years, pretending to be one Rabbi Lefkowitch. Then Arazi and his partner made their way to Egypt and using false names, joined the Jewish Brigade of the British army.

Ben-Gurion sent Arazi to Hotel Fourteen with a seemingly impossible mission: acquire those tanks, aircraft, and artillery. Ben-Gurion knew the truth. As it stood, the Haganah had enough ammunition to fight for three days. The Palmach, the Haganah's strike force consisted of three thousand fighters, several hundred of whom were women. Ben-Gurion well knew, as he noted later, that "you cannot hide a plane in a basement, nor a tank in an attic closet. What we had to do, therefore, was to try to buy them overseas . . . and hold them until the British troops would leave."

Arazi knew he and Rudolf Sonneborn had to be a team. Arazi sent some of his agents to Europe to see what weapons could be obtained, assuming he had the money.

Taking the name Albert Miller, Arazi rented an apartment on Central Park West, living apart from Hotel Fourteen because he did not want to be hampered by being monitored and because his private life was not a quiet one. Arazi was famous for being flamboyant, for giving out large amounts of money, for a very public presence. Elie Schalit, for one, was deeply concerned. The efforts in the United States were deliberately kept quiet. As the talk with J. Edgar Hoover had illustrated, there was almost a tacit agreement. The Haganah would very unobtrusively raise its funds and get its weapons, none of which would be used in or against the United States, in return for law enforcement mostly looking the other way.

There had been great hope placed not only in law enforcement but also in the government of the United States. The State Department Arabists, it was thought, might be obstructionist, but President Harry Truman would help. As it happened, such optimism was misplaced. On December 5, 1947, not even a week after the U.N. General Assembly had voted to partition Palestine into two nations, one Jewish and the other Arab, the United States announced an embargo on all arms sales to the Middle East. While such an approach had an appearance of fairness, with neither side getting weapons, in fact the Arabs had access to weapons from other sources and indeed had already bought $37 million worth of surplus arms from the United States, so the decision was devastating to the hopes of an independent Jewish state. Beyond American arms, Arabs also were getting arms from the British because of existing contractual obligations.

This reality stunned the Haganah representatives in New York and quickened the need for money and weapons. At its December 11 meeting, the Sonneborn Institute had seventy-two people in attendance. They were given a startling figure: they needed to raise $5 million by year's end. Even Sonneborn, always the optimist, was stunned. He knew that his members didn't have the necessary cash. But they were prominent American business people. Their names were good. They had the credit. They could borrow the money.

And then there was a disaster. On Saturday, January 3, 1948, an incident occurred that could have ended the entire Haganah effort in the country. The S.S. *Executor* was at Pier F in Jersey City. The ship was unloading its cargo. A wooden crate was headed toward the cargo deck. The day was cold and the work slow, making those on the pier anxious. The crate, swinging in the wind, suddenly split open. Its cargo fell all over the pier. The contents became evident: there were tins of TNT.

The police came, as did customs agents and the coast guard. Crates on the pier that were destined for Palestine were torn apart. Twenty-six of the crates contained TNT. Machinery in other crates appeared to be useful for the manufacturing of ammunition. A police captain noted that there was enough TNT to blow up "five Jersey Cities."

Phil Alper got a call immediately because Robert Keller, Alper's assistant, had seen it all. Someone was always on the dock when a shipment was about to be sent, and Keller had been the designated observer this time. Alper made a quick calculation. He had about four hours until the police or, more ominously, the FBI raided the apartment. All evidence had to be destroyed.

Keller arrived back at the apartment, and the two men got to work. They went back and forth. First, they called friends, and then they bundled. The friends ignored the ban on driving that wasn't essential. Alper gave rapid-fire orders. Bundles of sensitive papers were taken by people to their homes and hidden there until they were needed.

A prototype of the Gun was in the apartment. Alper, developing his skills on the spot, dismantled the weapon. There were also blueprints used for the Gun.

Suddenly, there was a knock at the door. There was no choice. Perhaps a raid was about to take place. The blueprints were rolled up and tossed out a window. They landed on a roof below.

The knocking stopped. Alper, wary of using the elevator, went down the stairs and headed to the most crowded place he could think of: Times Square. He went to three different hotels in the area, changing his location each night. Finally, he was sent to Washington to meet Elie Schalit.

The police, meanwhile, had traced the trucking company that had brought the TNT to the pier. From there, they located Alper's name and address. By then, however, there was nothing to find. Discreet inquiries were made to Mayor William O'Dwyer's office. O'Dwyer was deeply sympathetic to the Zionist cause. The New York police declared they had no interest in the case because the TNT had been found in New Jersey.

The New Jersey police had no one to charge. But there was more trouble. Demolition blocks that had been hidden on a farm were discovered. There was wild speculation that there was a traitor.

A strategy had to be developed. One had already worked at the Canadian border, and now it would be used again. The police would be given a solution to the mystery of the TNT, but the solution would stop at a low level. The other projects would not be put in jeopardy.

Alper, now in hiding with Schalit, received an order. He was to return to New York City. The headlines of January 15 screamed about the five men who had surrendered to the FBI and admitted guilt concerning the TNT. Twenty-three-year-old Philip Alper was noted to be the ringleader. Questioned by agents, Alper gave an impassioned speech about the desperate need of the Jews. The agents, thinking the entire enterprise criminal, were surprised.

The five men appeared before federal judge William Bondy. The federal prosecutor, John F. X. McGohey, noted that the defendants had voluntarily surrendered. He recommended that the bail be minimum. The arms embargo violation was never mentioned. The men were freed on a $1,000 bond and awaited action by a federal grand jury.

The incident on the Jersey City pier had another devastating effect beyond the loss of the TNT. American Jews became aware of what was happening in terms of weapons being smuggled. It became much harder to raise money to get those weapons.

There were opportunities to purchase weapons in Czechoslovakia and elsewhere, but money needed to be founded. Back in the Land of

Israel, David Ben-Gurion had all this on his mind. Money was needed for weapons, to be sure, but Ben-Gurion understood all too well that if the *Yishuv* was considered weak, the United Nations might back off its partition plan in favor of a trusteeship, with the United Nations controlling the land. This was a nightmare for Ben-Gurion; the Jewish State, the cause to which he had devoted his life, was within his grasp. He couldn't lose it.

Eliezer Kaplan, the treasurer of the Jewish Agency, had gone to the United States. He assessed that maybe, using all the resources available, the Jews might be able to raise somewhere between $10 and $25 million. That was half of what was needed.

Ben-Gurion was determined to go back to the United States himself to try to raise the money. But Golda Meir (still Meyerson) told him that he was indispensable in Palestine, that he was needed there but that she could go. Ben-Gurion argued with her at a cabinet meeting. Meir demanded a vote. The cabinet agreed with her. Eliezer Kaplan begged her to raise $5 million. He said he realized the figure was unrealistically high, but he thought it might be enough for some kind of down payment. No one thought even that sum was possible.

Meir didn't have time to return to her apartment to pack. She went to the airport with no luggage, her inadequate winter coat, her simple dress, and her fierce determination.

New York greeted her with its worst snowstorm in sixty years. Meir met with Rudolf Sonneborn and others. Everyone was worried about the effect of the TNT discovery, but there was consent that there was no alternative other than trying to raise the funds. Henry Montor arranged for Meir to speak in Chicago at a meeting of a non-Zionist group, the Council of Jewish Federations and Welfare Funds.

It was January 21, 1948. Meir was tired. This was an uncommon audience for her, fund-raisers instead of passionate Zionists. She wasn't on the schedule of speakers, and her presence wasn't even announced prior to her appearance. She didn't know how much the audience knew about the Land of Israel or cared about it. She couldn't rehearse her speech.

As she approached the microphone, Meir made a decision. However unlikely the necessary sum was, she was going to ask for what the Jewish people needed.

She told the assembled crowd that the Jewish people in the Land of Israel would fight to the end. "If we have arms to fight with, we will fight with them. If not, we will fight with stones in our hands."

The crowd listened carefully.

> I want you to believe me when I say that I came on this special mission to the United States today not to save seven hundred thousand Jews. During the last few years the Jewish people lost six million Jews, and it would be audacity on our part to worry Jews throughout the world because a few hundred thousand more Jews are in danger.
>
> That is not the issue. The issue is that if these seven hundred thousand Jews in Palestine can remain alive, then the Jewish people as such is alive and Jewish independence assured. If these seven hundred thousand people are killed off, then for centuries we are through with the dream of a Jewish people and a Jewish homeland.
>
> My friends, we are at war. There is no Jew in Palestine who does not believe that finally we will be victorious. That is the spirit of the country. . . . But this valiant spirit alone cannot face rifles and machine guns. Rifles and machine guns without spirit are not worth very much, but spirit without arms can, in time, be broken together with the body.
>
> Our problem is time. The question is what we can get immediately. And when I say immediately, I do not mean next month. I do not mean two months from now. I mean now. . . .
>
> We are not a better breed; we are not the best Jews of the Jewish people. It so happened that we are there and you are here. I am certain that if you were in Palestine and we were in the United States, you would be doing what we are doing there, and you would ask us here to do what you will have to do. . . .
>
> You cannot decide whether we shall fight or not. We will. . . . The decision is taken. Nobody can change it. You can only decide one thing: whether we shall be victorious in this fight or whether the

Arabs will be victorious. That decision American Jews can make. It has to be made quickly, within hours, within days.

And I beg of you: Don't be too late. Don't be bitterly sorry three months from now for what you failed to do today. The time is now.

The crowd wept openly. And then they gave. They wrote checks. And after that, they made pledges. They used their homes and businesses as collateral for bank loans so that the money could be received immediately.

That afternoon in Chicago, Golda Meir raised $25 million.

Astounded at this amazing woman's success, the leaders of American Zionism arranged for Meir to make additional talks. And so she went around the country. In Palm Beach, Florida, she thought the crowd with its furs and jewels wouldn't be able to understand the freezing Haganah soldiers on watch. But for perhaps the only time on the trip, Meir's instincts failed her. The crowd did care, and it too gave.

When Meir completed her mission in America, she had raised $50 million. She returned to Palestine.

David Ben-Gurion, the leader she had defied, greeted her arrival at Lydda airport with these words: "Some day, when history will be written, it will be said that there was a Jewish woman who got the money which made the state possible."

Meanwhile, work continued at Hotel Fourteen. Rabinovich had been called back, and Teddy Kollek, later the famed mayor of Jerusalem, took charge of the work operating from above the Copacabana. Conceiving of himself less a boss than as a coordinator, Kollek proved to be a popular leader.

He was also a good fund-raiser. In late May 1948, Kollek found himself in need of $1 million to purchase airplanes from Czechoslovakia. He had one day to raise the money. He and the Sonneborn Institute were used to getting money in a month or even several months, but to get it in a single day seemed like an impossible task. Kollek assessed all the wealthy people he had already gone to and determined that they would not be able to provide the funds. He then spoke to Joseph Shulman, someone Kollek had known for a long while. Shulman, a textile merchant, said, "I have a rich friend whom I have never approached. I don't think he's interested in Israel, but let's try."

William Levitt had just built the first Levittown. He had brilliantly applied the technique of mass-producing items to building houses. There were communities with a few models. Levitt's timing was perfect. The soldiers coming home started families and wanted to build their families outside New York City but not so far outside that they couldn't drive to their jobs or enjoy New York City's cultural, dining, and other pleasures. Beyond that, Levitt created what amounted to a new community. He had two profound insights. By creating a community with houses similar to each other, the new suburbanites immediately found friends like themselves and friends with whom their children could play. In addition, by pricing the homes for these middle-class families, Levitt had made a fortune.

Levitt had an office on Northern Boulevard in Manhasset, New York, and Shulman arranged for a meeting between Kollek and Levitt. Kollek faced the builder and decided he needed to be honest and direct, at least up to a point. Kollek began, "I am the head of the Haganah Mission, and I would like to borrow a million dollars. I can't tell you what it is for because that is top secret. We will pay it back within a year."

Levitt was very far from a fool. He understood perfectly that in saying that the reason for the loan had to remain a secret, the Haganah planned to use it for weapons. In a way, Kollek was protecting Levitt. The builder asked several questions, including an important one: "What do I get as security?"

Kollek replied, "Nothing more than a promissory note from the State of Israel."

This was, objectively, a very bad deal. The new State of Israel might not even exist in a few months. There was to be no interest. There was certainly no real guarantee that Levitt would ever get a dime of his money back.

Levitt recalled, "So I said okay and I gave him the million dollars."

Kollek met that night with Eliahu Epstein, the Israeli ambassador, and Oscar Gass, the economic adviser. The next morning, he brought Levitt a note from the "Provisional Government of Israel. Note Number One. One Million Dollars." Epstein had signed the note.

Eventually, Israel did, in fact, repay the $1 million.

Ever since his arrival, Kollek had adapted well to his job. Everyone had to deal with a post-TNT reality, including the Sonneborn Institute.

The institute held its regular Thursday meeting on January 27 at Hotel McAlpin with fifty-seven people in attendance. Clearly, everyone had the TNT incident in mind. Sonneborn discreetly waited until all the waiters had left the room, stood up, and said, "There has been a considerable speculation and discussion as to the future of this group." Sonneborn was absolutely clear that the work would continue as 1948 began. He noted that the date of the British army's withdrawal was less than four months away. At that moment, the Haganah would suddenly become a national army. It would not be fighting local Arabs and hiding from the British. It would be facing the might of a collected assault from Arab armies. If Sonneborn shared the common doubt that a Jewish ragtag group of soldiers could resist that attack, he didn't mention it. He did know that everyone capable of fighting would be drafted, and that meant a lot more supplies were needed. Sonneborn knew the institute's essential function was now shifting from simply supplying the money to buy weapons to getting the supplies themselves and getting them over to the Land of Israel.

Indeed, Teddy Kollek had drawn up a list of exactly what the Sonneborn Institute had to get. Sonneborn passed around copies of that list to those at the meeting.

The people present read over the three pages filled with the *Yishuv*'s staggering needs:

> Two million sand bags, one thousand tons of barbed wire, one hundred thousand feet of corrugated iron . . . ten thousand coats, ten thousand pairs of boots, ten thousand raincoats, two thousand rubber boots, forty thousand blankets, three thousand tents (for 2, 8, and 16 men), ten thousand cots, five hundred thousand emergency rations,

ten thousand canteens, ten thousand sweaters, thirty thousand pairs of socks . . . one thousand pairs of binoculars, one thousand compasses, one thousand telephones and five hundred miles of telephone cables, and fifty switchboards . . . one thousand jeeps, one thousand bicycles, two hundred motorcycles, fifty water trucks, twenty gasoline trucks, two hundred armored trucks, one thousand 2½ ton trucks, one thousand ¾ ton trucks . . . three hundred "light projectors" (searchlights), thirty drafting tables, two hundred Hebrew typewriters, ten English typewriters, a print shop, a multigraph machine, two hundred megaphone systems.

Sonneborn gave the members no time for doubts. A new nonprofit membership organization was to be established. It would be called Materials for Palestine, Inc. An office at 250 West Fifty-Seventh Street, Room 1905, was set up. The plan for an open operation instead of acting in secret meant that no materials that were embargoed or considered contraband would be obtained. All the materials had to be gathered and sent in a manner totally in line with American law. In essence, Materials for Palestine was just sending materials overseas as a family might send items to families in another country, although they were certainly not the sort of materials a family usually sent and not on the massive scale needed.

Materials for Palestine became a sort of clearinghouse. All over the country, people who had just about anything to give contacted the Materials for Palestine office. Isaac Imber, who helped direct merchandise to the office, corresponded with members of the Sonneborn Institute around the United States. He developed a pattern. He would write to each of the members and ask them to tell him the names of big surplus dealers in their area. The dealers kept track of what was available, and it was a lot, because the country was unloading a lot of war materials. Once Materials for Palestine was able to keep up with what was available, when an item was requested and located, an expert was sent out to evaluate it. No one asked too many questions about how a particular dealer obtained the goods.

Because of contacts through the institute, the goods were frequently free. When costs were involved, another method was used. A locally important person was contacted and asked to hold a meeting in the family home. A specific amount of money was mentioned. The person contacted other people sympathetic to the Zionist cause, held the meeting, and got the money overnight. The materials would then be bought and sent to the best port for shipment overseas.

Materials for Palestine needed to look in new directions for the necessary materials, so it hired Sam Sloan as its specialist to attend conventions and make friends. The idea behind this effort is that most of the heavy materials would not be shipped to New York City but would be in places around the country. As Sloan collected names of people, he cultivated contacts where the materials themselves were located. Conventiongoers were, like Sam Sloan himself, gregarious storytellers, backslapping, friendly people. The contacts knew lots of people in their home areas, and Sloan got regular calls about new shipments. For example, Sloan had contact with burlap bag dealers who imported sandbags from Calcutta. Sloan got 350,000 sandbags in a single afternoon. Those sandbags were used to protect a convoy opening a road to Jerusalem that was then under siege.

On February 27, Materials for Palestine sent out its first West Coast shipment: 350 sixteen-man tents, 1,701 steel helmets, and 2,000 helmet liners. Those helmets made their way to Haifa just in time for the Jews to use in the house-to-house fighting taking place in the city.

The requests came pouring in. Some must have seemed ridiculous to the people on Fifty-Seventh Street: records of Beethoven and Bach recordings, four Waring blenders (these were to be used to get rid of documents), and Ben-Gurion's own request of fifty volumes of sacred Jewish literature.

The fighting in Palestine quickened the pulses of those in America who were helping. Suddenly, Jews and Christians joined together in common cause to help an ancient nation be reborn. Those who had at one point declined to help now were eager to do so.

ORGANIZING FOR ACTION

The system for gathering all the required goods was matched by the methods used to ship the materials. Harris J. Klein, a member of the Sonneborn Institute, was an attorney who had a specialty in the trucking industry. He organized a trucking network that consisted of 150 separate truck lines. About three-quarters of the truck lines were owned by Jews, but the remaining ones included Gentile owners who were deeply committed to Israel. A Midwest trucker named Brady called one time. He had a question. He wondered "if there was any trouble" because "he'd only moved six loads that month."

Somehow in such a giant transportation system, there was always room in a truck to put goods Materials for Palestine had collected and transport them for free to Materials for Palestine warehouses that were located in Los Angeles, San Francisco, Chicago, Denver, New Orleans, and the principal warehouse at 177 Water Street in Brooklyn. Rusty Jarcho, who worked in the company's office, did all the routing for all the goods. It was a complex, demanding job. Jarcho compared the warehousing and shipping to Sears, Roebuck.

Sometimes, the Materials people weren't even sure where the goods came from. A stranger from Rock Hill, North Carolina, called with a question: "Could the Jewish army use good shockproof waterproof watches?" When he was told the watches could absolutely be used, he hung up. The watches began appearing a few days later. Eventually, more than three hundred watches arrived. The Materials people assumed that every Jewish jeweler in the South had been contacted and had helped.

A mobile hospital unit arrived from Philadelphia. GI knives, forks, and spoons came from Omaha.

A Christian woman in Pittsburgh approached a Jewish friend who belonged to the Sonneborn Institute and gave him fifty dollars to be used for the Haganah to get ammunition. He sent a letter explaining the story, along with his own check for $50,000.

Materials for Palestine shipped two thousand parachutes that it listed as hospital supplies. When questioned, the sender explained that field hospitals in the Negev were isolated and in danger from Arabs, so they could only receive supplies by a parachute drop.

Materials for Palestine received many offers of illegal goods such as airplane motors or a gelatin for flame throwers. But the group had to be careful. Their mandate was to stay completely legal, so they wrote polite letters to those who offered "black goods" declining the offers.

But the realities of the military situation that the Haganah faced didn't allow the organization the luxury of always obeying the law. Sometimes they had to speak quietly to supporters in search of goods they needed. And sometimes they got caught. Irving Norry of Rochester, New York, was an institute member. He was arrested in March 1948 and was charged with purchasing and then storing six thousand dynamite caps without having the necessary license. He pleaded guilty and received a suspended sentence. He never revealed why he wanted the caps.

A month earlier, in February, Phil Alper, Elie Schalit, and three others pleaded guilty to making false export declarations. Judge Sylvester J. Ryan gave them all a suspended sentence. Clearly knowing their real intentions, the judge declared: "You endeavored to provide means of defense to an otherwise helpless people. I do not regard you men as criminals." Neither did most Americans, who saw the Jews attempting to revive their ancient homeland as heroic.

Most Americans did not know the whole story, the acquisition of ships and planes, the political struggles, and all the rest. And all that was before a group of invading Arab armies tried to prevent the very birth of Israel.

4

PLANES AND SHIPS AND WEAPONS

During the same span of time as the effort to get materials of all kinds was under way, there were other important activities taking place in America.

Assessing the accomplishments and his outstanding needs, it was Jacob Dostrovsky who focused on the single greatest effort still required: ships were desperately needed to take survivors of the Shoah (the Holocaust) from displaced persons camps in Europe to the Land of Israel. Dostrovsky knew David Ben-Gurion's conclusion was completely correct. The Jews desperately needed people for the demographic war they were fighting with the Arabs. The Jews needed people to fight in the military war, in the economic war, in the war for people's approval. And, again as Ben-Gurion knew, no one else wanted these people. Ships were needed now. Every moment counted. Every suffering survivor needed help.

This special project required its own leader. Ben-Gurion sent a man named Danny Shind to oversee this effort. The redheaded Shind set up a dozen false companies and placed them in different locations. Each company would buy only a few ships, sail under different flags—usually Panamanian—across the Atlantic, and then make the effort to break the British blockade. (This effort will be discussed in chapter 6.)

Meanwhile, Shlomo Rabinovich was approached by a man with an incredible idea. Born in 1917, Adolph (Al) Schwimmer had been a transport pilot in World War II and a Trans World Airlines flight engineer flying between Cairo and Washington, DC. After the war, he started taking trips to Europe on business, and on one of the trips, his mother asked him if there were records of her family's fate. Schwimmer visited various displaced persons camps and discovered that most and perhaps all of his family had perished. By visiting the camps, Schwimmer also discovered that the Jews had no place to go. Schwimmer previously had almost no Jewish ties, and certainly he had no connection to Jews living a thousand miles away, working hard to fulfill an amazing dream of reestablishing their ancient nation in their ancient homeland.

Schwimmer was transformed. On one trip to New York, he made his way into Rabinovich's office at the Jewish Agency office in Hotel Fourteen and simply said, "I just wonder whether I can help."

Rabinovich was naturally suspicious of people who just walked in to the office and wanted to help. They could be plants, spies, people out to hurt the cause, or lunatics. But, however remote the possibility, they also might be extraordinarily helpful. And so the wary Rabinovich wanted to know why Schwimmer had come to the office. Schwimmer said he was emotionally affected by what was happening to the Jewish people as they sought to reestablish their nation. "I've been reading the newspapers," he said. "Airplanes might make a difference."

Rabinovich was astonished. Airplanes were an idea he hadn't considered because he couldn't imagine where the Haganah could get airplanes and if they got them, what they could do with them. It wasn't like they could hide airplanes in the back of a safe house in Tel Aviv as they might hide rifles or explosives. Besides, the Jews had virtually no pilots to fly any planes they might get. Even more, planes required an incredible support system that included airstrips, which there was almost no chance of building without being discovered, and other installations such as weather stations and repair facilities. In all, the very notion of planes seemed a very far-fetched idea. But Rabinovich had to admit, however far-fetched, it was enticing.

PLANES AND SHIPS AND WEAPONS

Rabinovich took down Schwimmer's name and then offered the usual suggestion, "Come in again, sometime." This request for another visit was to determine how serious a visitor might be, whether, for example, the enthusiasm would eventually be overcome by fear or some other emotion.

Schwimmer, though, was not a shy man. All through the summer months of 1947 and the turn to fall, Schwimmer kept returning to Hotel Fourteen, talking airplanes every time he was able to speak with someone. Rabinovich started asking him questions and even, quietly, had his background checked.

It was just then that Yehuda Arazi arrived in the United States. Rabinovich asked Schwimmer to speak with Arazi. Schwimmer later recalled, "My first take of him was that he was wearing suspenders and a belt. A guy even more cautious than Rabinovich."

But Schwimmer soon saw the real Arazi, a man whose limp served as a perfect metaphor for a daring man undaunted by risk.

Arazi told the American that the Federal Bureau of Investigation (FBI) would follow him and that he would be breaking both U.S. and international laws. He could lose his American citizenship. The State Department in particular was doing all it could to prevent the Jews from getting any arms, and the FBI was watching Hotel Fourteen. Schwimmer hadn't known that, but the grim reality did not even slow him down. He believed in himself. He believed, mostly correctly as it turned out, that he could stay a step ahead of the authorities because he was bold.

Arazi soon provided funds to Schwimmer, and the new recruit quit his job and together with his old friend Reynold (Rey) Selk headed to California to determine what sorts of planes were available. Once there, they drove out to the Lockheed plant to look at some Constellations, a plane Howard Hughes had helped design. The Constellations (nicknamed Connies by virtually all the pilots) could fly at three hundred miles an hour and had room for one hundred passengers.

Schwimmer flew back to New York only to discover that Arazi was undertaking a mission in Europe. Nahum Bernstein became Schwimmer's new contact. He gave Bernstein the details. It was possible to buy the Constellations for only $15,000 each. However, they really needed to be modified, Schwimmer told Bernstein, to meet the postwar requirements. That would be expensive; the planes would cost $200,000 each. Schwimmer thought they should buy three of the Constellations along with some smaller planes, ten C-46s.

Overwhelmed by the cost, Bernstein concluded it couldn't be done. Schwimmer, however, was no doubt familiar with an armed forces slogan from World War II: the difficult can be done immediately; the impossible takes a little longer. Schwimmer, the American, fit right in with a developing ethos from the new Jewish nation. There was a can-do attitude, a sense that there is always a way. And so Schwimmer offered an alternative. He could, he assured Bernstein, get together some mechanics. He needed Lockheed's technical knowledge and some space, and the mechanics could fix the planes themselves at a fraction of the cost.

Schwimmer got a check for $45,000, enough to pay for three Constellations to be delivered to Burbank, where they would be updated. Schwimmer returned to Burbank and opened an office. Schwimmer Aviation Service was in business.

Schwimmer recruited workers, experts, and pilots. He contacted old friends and pilots he had flown with. He met people who offered to help. His friend Sam Lewis took on the challenge of being the chief pilot and trained other pilots. Lewis, Schwimmer thought, could fly any plane ever built. A core team of pilots was eventually assembled.

It wasn't long before Ben-Gurion and the Haganah leaders in Tel Aviv found an invaluable use for the Constellations.

Michael Felix was second in command of Haganah. He and Ben-Gurion talked regularly. Felix had been born in Czechoslovakia and told Ben-Gurion that Otto Felix, his brother, had recently returned to the country of their birth in his work as a lawyer. Otto was amazed to discover that many of his university friends had become powerful government officials. Some were generals. The Czechs were selling surplus arms all over, including to Arab nations. Felix wanted to use his brother's contacts and asked Ben-Gurion about the possibility of doing so.

Ben-Gurion was intrigued and asked to meet with Otto Felix. But there was a problem. Ben-Gurion was always being disturbed, sometimes it seemed by everyone in the country. The idea of Czech arms was a matter that needed to be handled very delicately. Ben-Gurion needed quiet that he didn't have. And so he did the unthinkable. He asked Otto Felix to visit him on Yom Kippur, the holiest day of the Jewish year and the only day in the year when Ben-Gurion wouldn't be disturbed.

Felix eventually returned to his home country and very carefully negotiated an initial sale of forty-three hundred rifles, two hundred machine guns, and ammunition. There were to be future purchases as well. But Ben-Gurion knew there was another, seemingly impossible, obstacle. How could the Jews get the new weapons to their land?

At a meeting with Ben-Gurion and the Haganah leaders, someone brought up the Constellations as a way to transport the new military purchases. The great attraction of the planes was that they didn't have to break the British blockade. They could just fly over it, land on a secret airfield, and unload their cargo.

Plans were drawn up. Pilots were recruited. The weapons delivery was carefully planned in an operation code-named "Yakum Purkan." The name came from an ancient Aramaic prayer, translated as "salvation would be forthcoming from Heaven." The Constellations would indeed bring their own form of salvation from the bright blue skies over the Land of Israel.

Schwimmer had a friend named Marty B. Bellefond. He was a big, handsome guy who had flown with the air force. Bellefond had started World Airways, which he began by buying a single C-47 for $750 cash and the rest owed on a $15,000 purchase price. Bellefond ran his new company at Teterboro Airport in New Jersey from a tent that he rested next to a pay telephone booth from which he could receive and place calls. He had a profitable business until the airline authorities started going after him. Needing an alternative, Bellefond found himself in

New York City, wandering the Battery and looking at ships. He noticed several that flew Panamanian flags. Immediately, he thought that if ships could fly the flag, why couldn't there also be an airline that did so?

His wife replied that when she had been a student at Radcliffe College, she had been friends with Gilberto Arias, a student at Harvard University, whose uncle was the president of Panama. Bellefond called Arias that evening, and the Panamanian, by then a successful and well-connected attorney, liked the idea and invited Bellefond to visit the country. Bellefond hired Arias and eventually created LAPSA, the flag airline of Panama. Unfortunately, however, Bellefond was kicked out of World Airways by the other stockholders. He had a franchise from Panama but no airline with planes to fly.

It was then that he ran into Irvin "Swifty" Schindler.

Schindler had started an airline, Service Airways, that failed, but it was still registered as a company. Schindler had flown for the Air Transport Command during World War II and in 1944 had started Service Airways; when it failed, he found himself working for a company in which the chief pilot said he would never have a Jew serving as a captain. Unhappy and bored with his job, Schindler was looking for alternatives. During a layover in London, Schindler met with Irwin "Steve" Schwartz, a navigator for the same airline. Schwartz said he too was so disgusted with his experience with the airline that he had decided to leave flying altogether. He confided to Schindler that he had applied to be a radio operator on one of the ships that the Jews were using to smuggle Holocaust survivors into Palestine.

One day, Schindler got a call from Nahum Bernstein, who mentioned that he was "a friend of Steve's." Bernstein, ever the lawyer, wanted to make sure that Service Airways was both incorporated and remained legally registered. Satisfied, Bernstein said he had a business proposition to make. How would Schindler like to be president of a revived Service Airways, complete with three Constellations? Schindler's initial job would be to find some small work flying cargo to Europe until the planes were needed for their more serious mission. Suites

515 and 516 at 250 West Fifty-Seventh Street had a new tenant in a matter of days. Service Airways had been reborn.

Schwimmer, meanwhile, got Panamanian registry numbers for the planes, which were ready to leave Burbank.

Authorities had stumbled too late onto the plot of using the airplanes to provide supplies to the Jews in Palestine. The customs agents were sent to the airport to stop the planes from taking off. Schwimmer was not exactly a rule follower. He taxied the planes right at the customs agents and then got the planes off the ground.

While the planes were in Sicily waiting to fly to the Land of Israel, one of Charles "Lucky" Luciano's men came to investigate. Luciano had been deported to Italy from the United States, but he had not given up his criminal ways.

The pilots explained who they were, and the henchman was very relieved that they were not after his boss. He asked them if the Jews needed anything for their fight. They told him they had an immediate need for Thompson submachine guns. The next day, a case of the guns was delivered to the pilots.

When the weapons from Czechoslovakia were eventually delivered, the Haganah soldiers were shaken. The Czechs had confiscated an enormous amount of Nazi weaponry, and so there were Israeli soldiers in the Negev who looked down at their rifles and saw the German eagles with which the Nazis stamped their weapons. It turned out that the irony of Jews using Nazi weapons to stop Arabs trying to kill Jews was not enough to stop the soldiers.

The Czechs also sold Schwimmer defective Messerschmitt airplanes. Undaunted, the pilots repaired the planes and learned to use them.

When they got to the Land of Israel, one of the pilots, Lou Lenart, came up with an interesting plan. Like the British during the Second World War, the Jews in Israel were extraordinarily vulnerable to air attack. Egyptian planes would fly over unimpeded, drop bombs, and then fly low to strafe the people below. Lenart came up with a plan to attack the Egyptian planes in secret while they were still on the ground. While preparing for the attack, however, Lenart and the other pilots were confronted with another, more immediate and more serious problem. Six thousand Egyptian troops were at the outskirts of Tel Aviv. They consisted of seven infantry battalions, about six hundred various vehicles, and their own advanced antiaircraft weapons. If the Egyptians were able to capture Tel Aviv, the war would be over. The Egyptians would overrun Israel.

Lou Lenart became the first leader of an Israeli Air Force attack as it went after the advancing Egyptians. On the way there, his plane along with the other three passed over Israelis who thought they were enemy planes and began to attack them with antiaircraft fire. Dodging the fire, the pilots got to the Egyptian troops.

As Lenart approached, the guns malfunctioned. The bomb releases didn't work properly. Lenart looked to his left and right and didn't see anyone. Lenart dropped a seventy-kilogram bomb onto a group of trucks with surrounding troops bunched together in Ishdud's town square.

Lenart made three passes over the Egyptian tanks and troops. When he knew he needed to get closer to shoot at them, he flew his plane upside down. The Egyptians were completely surprised by the air attack. Israeli intelligence agents intercepted an Egyptian dispatch sent from the brigade commander back to Cairo: "We were heavily attacked by enemy aircraft and we are scattering." The Egyptians were convinced that the four Israeli planes were an advance group, that the Israelis had thousands of planes waiting, ready to attack.

The four planes had stopped the Egyptian movement forward, and Tel Aviv was saved. Unfortunately, Eddie Cohen, a South African volunteer, went down in the fight, but the three other pilots—Lenart, Modi Alon, and Ezer Weizman—returned safely.

And Lenart's original attack plan was not forgotten. During the 1967 war, Israel destroyed almost three hundred Egyptian planes on the ground.

Lenart was not the only American to fight in Israel's War of Independence.

PLANES AND SHIPS AND WEAPONS

Dr. Ruth Westheimer was not then an American, much less a famous therapist. After her parents had been murdered by the Nazis, Westheimer, who had been sent to Switzerland before her father and mother had been taken captive, decided that she would make aliyah, and go to the Land of Israel. She joined the Haganah. Her small size (she was four foot seven) was useful in the military effort and she became both a scout and a sniper. During Israel's War of Independence, Westheimer was near an exploding shell and suffered from a serious wound that left her unable to walk for several months.

Milton Rubenfeld had been a pilot both for the Royal Air Force and the U.S. Army during World War II. He was approached by one of Al Schwimmer's colleagues to determine if Rubenfeld would be willing to fly for Israel. Rubenfeld, an adventurer if there ever was one, agreed. In early 1948, he flew transport missions.

Later, in Czechoslovakia, he became one of the combat flyers (along with his co-American Lou Lenart) actually flying. On May 14, 1948, Rubenfeld along with four other pilots made up the entirety of the Israeli Air Force. He couldn't fly with the other pilots on May 29, 1948, the day Eddie Cohen's plane went down. There had been only four planes for the five pilots, and Rubenfeld had to stay behind.

Rubenfeld would soon have his chance. Twelve hours after the first fight, Rubenfeld and Weizman took off in the only two planes left that were capable of flying. Rubenfeld's fighter was hit, but he got the plane back to Israeli territory. He bailed out from twelve thousand feet while he was still over the Mediterranean Sea. Because his parachute opened just as he hit the sea, he sustained various injuries, including three broken ribs. He was still several miles offshore. He began to swim, and for a couple of hours, his strength held up. He realized he couldn't go any further. And then he realized, "The water was only up to my knees. I'd been swimming for hours in the water. I could have stood up at anytime. I didn't realize it because I was so far out. The farmers . . . were shooting at me as I was coming out of the water. They thought I was an Arab pilot." The farmers didn't even know an Israeli Air Force existed, and so they began their shooting. Rubenfeld could not speak

Hebrew and barely knew a few words in Yiddish. Struggling to convince them that he was Jewish, he started yelling out the only Jewish words that came to his mind: "Shabbos, gefilte fish."

Rubenfeld eventually returned to the United States. In 1988, he and his wife appeared as characters in the movie *Big Top Pee-wee*. The movie starred Paul Reubens in his Pee-wee Herman character.

There may have been some nepotism involved in the casting. Milt Rubenfeld was Pee-wee Herman's father.

Of the many Americans who fought in Israel, without doubt David "Mickey" Marcus became the most famous.

Marcus, born on the Lower East Side in New York, had attended West Point and had served in the U.S. Army during World War II. On December 9, 1947, Marcus was a lawyer in New York. It was then, acting on Ben-Gurion's orders, that a Haganah agent named Major Shlomo Shamir approached Marcus, asking for help finding an officer to advise the Jewish Agency. Together they approached various people, but it was soon clear no one could be found. By January 1948, Mickey Marcus, realizing that only he could fulfill this role, accepted a position with Shamir. Marcus's agreement thrilled Shamir, but he was puzzled. "Why are you so willing to leave your office and your profession and your wife and your home to help a new, little country to which you owe no allegiance?"

Marcus looked at Shamir and said, "Have you been to Dachau, Major? Have you ever seen and heard a group of Jewish skeletons singing Hatikvah? Have you ever stood and cried as I was crying then and as I am crying now, shedding tears which were and are at one and the same time tears of anger, tears of pride, and tears of joy?"

And so they went to Palestine, with Marcus assuming the name Michael Stone. He was needed as the chief instructor in the new Israeli Army. He began by having American military publications translated into Hebrew. He established schools to train officers. He planned military strategy and tactics. He visited the Haganah forces on virtually every battlefront. He wasn't surprised to see a total lack of leadership. In the three months he was there, he set about to transform the Haganah into a fighting army. It was under his command that work began on a bypass road to break the siege of Jerusalem.

Ben-Gurion got Marcus's report on what he had seen and done. A day later, Ben-Gurion wrote to a Haganah representative in the United States that "the expert who came here with Shlomo completed his examination of our units; his report is very brilliant, and he understands well our special situation." Ben-Gurion continued, asking for "at least ten like Marcus."

It was crucial for Marcus to hide his true identity from the British. Once he and Ben-Gurion were driving together to a meeting. Their vehicle was stopped by a British patrol. Ben-Gurion was very nervous. The British officer wanted to know Marcus's name. Without hesitation and in a calm voice, Marcus said, "Michael Stone." The British officer was still suspicious. "And what is your occupation?" Again, Marcus didn't hesitate. "I'm a foundry worker." Marcus's misshapen nose, the result of one too many poundings during his boxing career, did indeed give him the appearance of being a tough foundry worker. Marcus then pulled out his identification. The forgery was excellent, made seemingly real by the fact that the papers looked well worn.

The officer let them pass.

Only after they were clear of the British did Marcus remember what he had on the third finger of his left hand. He told Ben-Gurion, "It's my West Point ring with my real name engraved inside."

Marcus took off his ring and never wore it again.

On June 9, 1948, the forces were calming down. The Arabs and the Israelis would have a cease-fire that would take effect on the following day. The long-awaited armistice would take place at ten the next morning. Mickey Marcus was staying at the central front headquarters of the Palmach, which was the Israeli Army's strike force. This headquarters was located several miles west of Jerusalem in the Arab village of Abu Ghosh. That evening, Marcus spoke at length with Yigal Allon, the leader of the Palmach.

Marcus was enthusiastic and excited. The dream of a Jewish state in Israel was about to become a reality. Unable to sleep, Marcus rose in the middle of the night and went for a walk. He began his return at 3:50 a.m.

A sentry guarding the headquarters saw a man approaching in the dark. Most soldiers in the Palmach spoke English, but as it happened this sentry did not. Marcus spoke no Hebrew. There was immediate confusion. Marcus began to explain his rank. The sentry, confused and scared, heard English and believed Marcus was an English officer attached to the Arab Legion of Jordan. The sentry fired a shot. Mickey Marcus fell down dead hours before the cease-fire was scheduled to begin.

Marcus was laid to rest at West Point.

David Ben-Gurion sent a wire to Marcus's widow:

> In the short time he had been with us—too short, alas!—he succeeded in making an outstanding contribution to the history of the days in which the State of Israel came into being.
>
> As a man and a commander he endeared himself to all who came in contact with him, and his fame spread throughout all ranks of our armed forces. They all admired his superb courage, his remarkable military intuition, his unlimited devotion, and his natural spontaneous human fellowship.
>
> His name will live forever in the annals of the Jewish people.

Before all this fighting in the Land of Israel, the future Jewish state, as discussed, needed planes. Al Schwimmer knew that the Israelis needed bombers. He therefore bought two B-17 bombers on the condition that he turn them into scrap metal. Of course, he had no intention of doing that. But after Schwimmer had legally purchased the bombers, he was informed that he could not take possession of them. One of the planes was at an airfield in Tulsa, Oklahoma. Schwimmer went there in uniform with a friend, walked onto the field, got into the plane, and flew off. The tower desperately tried to call the plane, but Schwimmer ignored what was said and took his plane into the skies.

All the planes that Schwimmer and the others got required trained pilots. Steve Schwartz, who had joined the newly revived Service Air-

PLANES AND SHIPS AND WEAPONS

ways, was given the task of recruiting pilots. He relied in part on a general effort, yet another in the myriad of organizations, this one started by Teddy Kollek.

Land and Labor for Palestine had what was in one sense an old job, which was to recruit people to work in the Land of Israel. The new organization set up its headquarters at the Hotel Breslin at Twenty-Ninth Street and Broadway.

Land and Labor for Palestine had an interesting method for finding new recruits. Through Materials for Palestine, Land and Labor got World War II chaplaincy records. Every Jewish soldier in World War II was listed. The information included name, rank, branch of service, and a home address, which very likely was still where that soldier lived. The Jewish men and women on the list were invited to a talk about life for Jews in Palestine. Those who expressed some interest received a letter that read: "We have been informed that you are interested in lending assistance to Palestine. We should like to discuss this matter with you. Please telephone this office for an appointment."

Those who responded to the letter and made an appointment heard a speaker. All the speakers to all the individuals or groups that came to the office spoke the same words:

> The struggle for Palestine needs manpower. Struggle doesn't necessarily mean fighting. Labor, to provide food and other necessities, is not less important. The aims and objectives of Land and Labor for Palestine are to encourage and assist individuals interested in strengthening and developing the Jewish Homeland by providing technical and agricultural skills. Land and Labor for Palestine is the official body deputed to advise individuals as to the needs of Palestine and the procedure recommended. . . . The need is for people of integrity with an urgent desire to assist, to the utmost of their capacity, for the duration of the present emergency in Palestine. Volunteers are needed who can adjust themselves to a new environment, rugged living conditions, and who are ready to do any kind of hard labor. . . . The minimum stay required is two years, or the emergency to be determined by the Palestinian authorities.

The speakers received special training. The potential recruits were needed, and there could be no mistakes in talking with them. The training included these directions:

> The technique of speaking shall be a cold, factual presentation of the subject matter. . . . It should be made clear to the audiences that Land and Labor for Palestine is operating as a perfectly legal organization. At the same time, it must be emphasized that careless talk, based upon misunderstanding of highly emotional individuals, may result in misinterpretation, also rumors, and thereby endanger our project.

The applicants were not told in the initial interviews whether or not they had been accepted for the program. This way, any spies could not determine the criteria Land and Labor was using to choose recruits. Those conducting interviews asked a variety of very carefully considered questions. These included:

> Why are you anxious to offer your services on behalf of Palestine?
> Do you expect to make any financial gain in this project?
> Are you prepared to do any kind of job that may be required of you, even though it may involve hard, dirty work?
> Would you be ready to perform a task that is not the sort of work that you have been doing?
> Are you prepared to accept primitive living conditions?
> Will you accept orders and instructions without question?

There was a required medical examination, and sometimes, at the discretion of the examiner, a candidate was also sent to a psychiatrist.

Those applicants who were accepted followed a strict procedure. The first step was to get a passport application from the State Department passport office nearest to the applicant's house. Help was available in filling out the passport applications.

These were the directions for those helping the applicants with their passport applications:

The applicant will give his destination as either Scandinavia, Holland, Belgium, France, or Switzerland. In order to be able to give advice as to what ships sail to these countries, where those ships travel, from where they leave, etc., the local passport person should familiarize himself with the sailings of various lines, information which can be procured at any travel bureau.

When giving advice, he [that is, the local person giving the advice] should keep in mind the following:

Don't give too many the same story.

Don't send too many down to the Passport Office on any given day.

Applicants for a passport had to fill out a question about the purpose of their trip. Here those helping the applicants had to be concerned. Originally, applicants had written down that they wished to travel to Palestine, but soon enough those applications were denied by the State Department. And so alternatives were needed. Some possibilities included "to visit relatives" if the applicant in fact had any relatives in Western Europe, "to tour, vacation, or trip. If a soldier who served in the ETO, the applicant can say: to visit a friend, or his girl; he must NEVER say for a job or education unless the applicant has actual proof that a job really awaits him. As the summer months roll around, hundreds will be preparing to go for their vacations abroad."

As those helping applicants evaluated results, they made various changes. For example, organizers of this effort noted that military-age young men with Jewish names were being denied a passport if they said they were going on vacation. It was decided that from then on, the applicants should list that they were going on business trips.

Materials for Palestine also played a role. They had business contacts overseas, and those contacts provided letterheads. Eventually, forty overseas companies agreed to provide letters saying the company had business dealings with the applicant.

With their passports in hand, the volunteers began a waiting period. Eventually, however, word came of their upcoming trip. Then they had to travel first to New York. Some of these men, secretly dubbed "specialists," were the most valuable. They had combat experience, for example, or some special skill needed by the Haganah. There was a higher number of these than might be expected from a random sample of the American population because applicants had to be males between the ages of eighteen and thirty-five, which meant that many of them had served during World War II. The others, dubbed "regulars," were the volunteers who had not participated in combat.

The specialists were asked to meet with "the Panel." This panel met at night in an office on Fourth Avenue. One of its members was a tank commander for General George S. Patton. Another had been on General Dwight D. Eisenhower's staff.

The applicants (the term *volunteer* was avoided because of the military connotations of the word) would arrive in New York to await being shipped overseas. The most trusted specialists picked up tickets for the sailings and distributed the tickets to the others. Then the applicants would get on a train to a Land and Labor camp in Peekskill, New York. Again wishing to mask their true intentions, the word *camp* was avoided in written and spoken communications. The word *seminar* was its substitute.

Once at the camp, the applicants heard lectures on the history of the Jews in Palestine and a description of the life there. Close-order drills began each day, and the men got used to the Hebrew commands barked at them.

The applicants received another interview from a Land and Labor representative at the seminar. After that, they filled out a form detailing the specifics of their military experiences. Five copies of this form were distributed, including one to Tel Aviv.

Eventually, the men left, usually by ship, and landed in various ports, including Le Havre in France. They were told to look for a man at the port carrying a book, which considering their plans, had an ironic title. The book was Ernest Hemingway's *A Farewell to Arms*. The greeter at the port got them on a train bound for Paris. From there, they were put on a train to Marseilles. Once they reached Marseilles, they boarded a bus that took them to the Grandes Arenas camp for displaced persons.

The camp was just outside the city. There they would wait with the other displaced people for ships to take them to Palestine.

Land and Labor workers meeting with the applicants had a particular interest in mind, although the workers did their best to mask that special interest. The interviewers were asked to pay particular attention to those with aviation experience. Without betraying their excitement, the interviewers had to dig deeper into the experiences of those who had been involved with aviation. Again, instructions for the interviewers were given. Beyond being available three weeks after acceptance, the applicants had to meet other sought-after requirements. These requirements were explicitly spelled out:

> Pilots. Ex-military (check Log Book and AAF Form 5). Commercial (at least 1,000 hours total time of which at least 100 twin-engined work with valid CAA license. See Log Book.).
> Navigators. Ex-military (at least 500 hours; should include celestial navigation. Check Form 5.).
> Flight radio operators. Minimum 500 hours. (Check Form 5. Should hold appropriate FCC license.).

For applicants who were found acceptable, a small amount of money was promised, and the applicant was given a ticket to New York. The applicant also got a piece of paper with a telephone number on it. When in New York, the applicant was to call the number and ask for "Sam." The number connected, of course, to Land and Labor, and the person answering would arrange a meeting for that evening. A representative from Land and Labor went to the meeting, asked even more questions, and explicitly mentioned the work that needed to be done in the Land of Israel. If the applicant passed this final interview, he was asked to go to the offices of Service Airways.

These pilots desperately needed additional airplanes, and the Haganah representatives were constantly searching for any that were available.

It was during a normal Thursday meeting of the Sonneborn Institute that a surplus dealer who was visiting New York from Indianapolis whispered about there being "everything you need" in a yard in Hawaii. Nathan Liff hardly looked the part of an international conspirator. The small, even-tempered owner of the Universal Airplane Salvage Company had glasses and gray hair. His company purchased surplus naval aircraft and melted down their aluminum parts. A large part of his business was in Hawaii. No, he responded to the normal question, he didn't know what was available.

Al Schwimmer got the information, but he and Rey Selk couldn't find the time to go to Hawaii themselves. Selk, though, had an idea. His cousin Hank Greenspun was living in Las Vegas, running a radio station.

Herman Milton Greenspun had been born in Brooklyn in 1909. His family was poor, and he grew up in a rundown neighborhood in New Haven, Connecticut. His mother, a former bootlegger, ran the family store. She was the one who taught him a lesson in self-defense he carried with him throughout his life. As a child, Greenspun worked hard delivering newspapers. One day he came to collect the money owed him by a neighbor. Instead of paying, the neighbor hurled anti-Semitic insults at the young boy. Greenspun returned home without the money and told his mother what had happened. She immediately marched him right back to the neighbor's house. Once the man opened the door, Greenspun's mother began to slap him over and over. Greenspun kicked him in the shins. There was no problem the next time Greenspun tried to collect what was owed him. "The episode taught me a lesson I would never forget: cowards generally avoid a target that hits back." After working as a criminal defense lawyer, Greenspun discovered he had no taste for defending people he was convinced were guilty. From there, he went into business until the army drafted him. Greenspun received four battle stars. General Eisenhower gave him a commendation.

After the war, in 1946, a friend of Greenspun's named Joe Smoot convinced him to go to Las Vegas to help Smoot with a racetrack. Once there, Greenspun made the city his home.

Greenspun was thirty-seven in March 1947 when he was hired by Benjamin "Bugsy" Siegel to work in publicity for Siegel's Flamingo Hotel. Greenspun only stayed in the job until June; Bugsy Siegel was murdered.

Greenspun was the very definition of the kind of tough and able guy the Haganah needed. He agreed to take some time off and head to Hawaii. He immediately reported back that Nathan Liff had been correct. The salvage company was located at Iroquois Point, Oahu's naval air station. There were, Greenspun gleefully reported, all kinds of planes, a wide variety of plane parts, armaments, communications equipment, and engines just lying around in piles or loaded into crates.

With the help of Willie Sosnow, a Brooklyn mechanic, Greenspun spotted exactly what he wanted, a pile of .30- and .50-caliber airplane machine guns. Greenspun checked the guns and was amazed that they were essentially new. On another field, there was yet another pile of machine guns, and there was a third pile in a "dump" run by the navy. Those guns, however, had not yet been declared as surplus because they were brand-new, and they were under guard by two marines.

Greenspun and Sosnow, claiming time pressures, said they had to stay on the field. Once the workers were gone, the two men rushed to the guns, picked out the best ones, took off the dust, dismantled them, and covered them with hydraulic brake fluid, which would prevent any further rusting. Then they put the guns into engine crates, weighting the crates to match the weight listed on the outside of the crate. The experienced Greenspun was still not pleased. He knew that the gun barrels would burn during the raging heat of battle. The navy dump had hundreds of such barrels as part of the war's surplus.

The two guards were intimidating. Greenspun watched them carefully. He noticed that as they made their rounds, there was an eight-minute gap every two hours when both guards were away from the barrels. Greenspun had picked up the gambler's instincts from living in Las Vegas, or perhaps he moved there because he already had it. In either case, eight minutes had to be enough.

Spotting his opportunity, Greenspun drove a fork lift to the dump, picked up some cases of the barrels, and returned, all within his eight minutes of opportunity.

By the end of their second week of work, Greenspun and Sosnow had loaded sixteen crates with machine guns and extra barrels. These were mixed in with crates containing legitimate airplane engines. The fifty-eight crates were loaded onto a plane and headed off to California.

Once all this material, which consisted of fifteen tons of machine guns, arrived to California, it had to be hidden before it could be shipped to Mexico and then on to Israel. Rey Selk was put in charge of hiding the guns. He was concerned because the FBI was asking questions in Hawaii. Selk's first move was to remove the guns from the crates. The crates were then burned, making discovery impossible, and the guns were dismantled. The guns were cleaned and oiled by volunteers organized by Bernard Fineman, a film producer in Hollywood. They were repacked in gunnysacks. Using Fineman's Beverly Hills penthouse suite, which served as the Haganah's West Coast headquarters, Selk and Fineman then began making phone calls. They each had friends. They had relatives. They had business contacts. Somehow they found space for the gunnysacks in this person's warehouse and that person's factory. Some people hid them in garages in very fancy neighborhoods.

Hank Greenspun was then called into action. Having gotten the guns out of Hawaii, his new job was to get them to Mexico. Greenspun found his way to Newport Beach, California, south of Los Angeles. There he began to make contact with people who had yachts available for charter. He wondered if any of them were available to run guns to Mexico. It was a bold move, pure Greenspun in its nature. The charter yachts were run by independent men, hard, eager for bookings, and excited by adventure and danger. Some yachts considered Greenspun's offer and declined. It was a dangerous mission, and they didn't want to chance breaking American law and getting caught. The potential consequences for them, their yacht, and their business were just too dangerous to take the chance, no matter what the compensation.

Lee Lewis, however, found the offer tempting. Lewis, formerly a merchant marine officer, had served with a tuna fleet as a navigator. He had saved enough so that he could eventually buy the *Idalia*, seventy-five feet of attractive vessel with teak paneling, five expansive cabins, and a majestic main mast measuring ninety-eight feet. The vessel had once been owned by Painless Parker, a dentist famous for his extravagant advertising.

Lewis had just returned from Acapulco, and so he was familiar and comfortable with the run to Mexico. Greenspun wished him to return right back there. Lewis heard the offer and recalled that he felt "very willing. I was imbued with the idea of sailing and adventure, and the combination of that with doing something for Palestine appealed to me."

Meanwhile, the U.S. Customs Service was right behind them. They had located and seized the shipment of airplane engines out of Hawaii and quickly realized that sixteen crates were missing. Greenspun and two companions, Soslow and Leo Gardner, a pilot who worked for Al Schwimmer, loaded the gunnysacks filled with machine gun parts onto a truck and headed for San Pedro, Los Angeles' port. The *Idalia* met them there and loading began. The machine gun parts were first put on a Higgins landing craft, where they were taken to Warren Newmark's Yacht Center. It was just before midnight, but the yacht's lights could not be used. The loading had to be done by candlelight. Before loading even began, the men had to get the sacks to the yacht. The problems began when the three men began lifting the sacks to load onto the Higgins barge. They quickly discovered an unpleasant truth. As Gardener noted, "It must have been low tide because the Higgins was way down from the side of the dock and each sack of guns had to be handed down and handed down and handed down. The guns had been packed five or six to a sack. Well, you can't put half a dozen fifty-caliber machine guns in a sack and lift it." Since there were about a hundred sacks, it didn't take long for the loaders to become exhausted.

And getting the sacks onto the barge wasn't the last of the problems. The Higgins had to sneak past a coast guard patrol. Once it got to the yacht center, the heavy sacks had to be lifted up from the Higgins and then taken down the *Idalia*'s winding staircase.

As the loading began, the railing broke. The yacht began to sink lower and lower. The yacht itself weighed thirty-four tons. Fifteen additional tons were being loaded onto it. With the boat half submerged, the portholes began leaking.

Lee Lewis took a look at his beloved vessel, his livelihood and his dream, and announced that he wasn't going to proceed. He told Greenspun that the vessel was not fit to make the voyage, and they wouldn't make it all the way to Acapulco. Lewis demanded that the guns be taken off the yacht immediately. Greenspun and Lewis began to argue, going back and forth loudly. Eventually a compromise was reached. Lewis would take the cargo to Catalina, where another ship would take it the rest of the way.

With Lewis at the wheel, the yacht went past the lighthouse that stood at San Pedro harbor's entrance and was on its way into the channel.

Hank Greenspun then pulled out a Mauser and ordered Lewis to turn over the wheel to one of the crew that Greenspun had brought along. Greenspun spoke in a blunt voice: "There is no boat waiting for us at Catalina. The *Idalia* is going all the way to Acapulco."

Lewis, furious that someone had taken control of his boat, stormed off to get some sleep. When he awoke, he noted that the boat hadn't gone very far. He heard the crew fighting among themselves and the angry Greenspun barking at them. Somehow all the provisions that were supposed to be loaded on the boat had been left on the dock. There was no food except for marshmallow cookies, stale bread, and canned sardines. There was no compass to be found, and the inexperienced crew couldn't figure out how to let out more sail, which impeded gathering any speed. Lewis, evidently wanting the voyage over, let out the sail and began his work again at the wheel.

He hadn't surrendered.

> I decided that sooner or later the others would fall asleep and I would again be master of my own vessel. By dusk we'd be in a

position where I could head the boat into the Coronado channel near San Diego. I remembered very clearly that there was a big bell buoy in the middle of the channel. I thought my best bet would be to jump off the boat and swim to the buoy, where a fishing boat would pick me up in the morning. Before going overboard I would lash the wheel and head the boat toward Coronado, where it would crash on the rocks. The first part worked out fine, just as I planned. I was about to slip over the side when I found I couldn't do it.

That was the turning point of the whole trip. Greenspun probably doesn't realize it, probably never knew it. The overwhelming factor was that I couldn't abandon my ship and destroy it. The second factor was I felt those guns ought to get to Palestine.

After some additional difficulties, the *Idalia* reached Acapulco after eleven days of not very smooth sailing. Lewis went to stay with a friend, and Greenspun went to arrange for the transfer of the arms.

Eventually, both Lewis and Greenspun, as well as others, would be arrested and tried. The FBI had gathered information over the years, thousands of pages of information on Greenspun alone, and finally indictments were ready.

Charlie Winters was sentenced in January 1949. Winters, a Protestant, had sold three B-17s to Al Schwimmer and then had recruited a crew and flown one of the planes himself. He had been found guilty of illegally exporting the B-17s and was sentenced to eighteen months in prison.

Al Schwimmer decided he wouldn't stay hidden from the law. He had already faced some close calls. At one point in 1948, Schwimmer was conducting a meeting at the Henry Hudson Hotel in New York. Suddenly, he heard that FBI agents were in the lobby looking for him. The agents headed up to his room in the elevator. Schwimmer charged down twenty flights of stairs, got into a car, and he and some friends headed for the Canadian border.

Schwimmer was in Israel in 1949 when he decided to return to the United States and go on trial in Los Angeles with others, including Lewis, for violating the Neutrality Act. Nahum Bernstein was there for the defense. Bernstein had made a deeply personal decision. He didn't know the government's case and was concerned about how far the investigation had gone. Bernstein didn't want any such investigation to reach Israel, and so he had decided that, if necessary, he would take personal responsibility for the decision to export the planes. But that wasn't necessary. The incredible precautions taken to separate one function from another had held, and unsurprisingly it was very difficult for any investigator to put the various pieces into the shape of an explanatory puzzle. The trial ended in February 1950. The background and context are important in order to understand the verdict. By the beginning of 1950, Israel had been declared a state, fought a war of independence and won it, and was widely admired in the United States, especially after the horrors of the Holocaust became more widely known to the governing leaders and the general public. Schwimmer, along with Rey Selk, Leo Gardner, and Service Airways, were all found guilty. They each received a fine of $10,000 but were not sentenced to any prison time. They were stripped of some civil rights. Schwimmer was no longer allowed to vote or hold a federal job and was forced out of the air force reserves.

Hank Greenspun, meanwhile, was also put on trial in a federal court, pleaded guilty to smuggling arms abroad the *Idalia*, and also received a fine of $10,000 without getting any prison time.

The Protestant Charlie Winters was ironically the only person in the entire underground effort to serve a prison term.

Greenspun was pardoned by President John F. Kennedy in 1961.

Schwimmer, meanwhile, had moved to Israel and started Israel Aircraft Industries. His day-to-day life was unaffected by his sentence, and therefore he was not concerned about a pardon. "I was never prepared to say I did something wrong. That's why I refused to ask to be pardoned for things I did back then." And then in 2001, Schwimmer was contacted by Brian Greenspun, a newspaper publisher in Las Vegas and, more importantly, Hank Greenspun's son. Brian Greenspun had attended law school with President Bill Clinton and petitioned Clinton for a pardon that did not include the need for an apology. Several weeks later, Al Schwimmer received his pardon without having to express any regrets.

In all, the acquisition of planes, ships, and weapons by the Haganah underground in the United States was remarkably successful. The effort had the support of literally thousands of Americans who were horrified by revelations about the Holocaust and were inspired by the efforts of a relatively small group of brave Jews to rebuild the life of the Jewish people by refounding their national home. There was a widespread sense that the Jews in Palestine faced an enormous challenge. The State Department was convinced, for example, that the Jews could not survive. And yet despite a general sense of doubt, the underground supporters were not despondent. The necessity of action kept despair away. They ignored the dreadful possibilities that reality might offer and focused instead on the meaning of their own efforts. Danger, fear of imprisonment or fine, the disapproval of anyone else, all these ceased to matter. They had found a mission after the overwhelming sense of powerlessness they had felt. The acquisition of weapons was, in some deep psychological respect, an acquisition of arms that they hadn't been able to undertake against the Nazis.

As it happened, the Haganah was not the only group from the Land of Israel to seek help for the self-defense of the Jewish people.

Another group, in an entirely separate enterprise, stood up to make sure that the people of Israel would live.

5

THE IRGUN'S WAY

The Haganah was not the only Jewish paramilitary movement in the Land of Israel. The Irgun Zeva'i Le'umi (often referred to by its Hebrew abbreviation of Etzel) was founded in 1931. Several Haganah commanders were strongly opposed to the Haganah's policy of self-restraint in fighting the Arabs and the British, who controlled the land after they were given a mandate following the First World War. The Irgun felt ideologically attached to Revisionist Zionism, which had been founded by Vladimir Jabotinsky. He had developed a coherent understanding of Zionism that included several central principles. These were that a vital effort was needed to bring all Jews to Palestine immediately, that the Arabs would not be restrained in their attacks except if each attack was met by an immediate retaliation, and that a Jewish nation could only be established through the use of military force. The rejection of restraint compelled the Irgun to carry out reprisal raids against the Arabs. These raids were opposed by both the Haganah and the Jewish Agency, the official political leaders of the Land of Israel, and so there was intense political rivalry and competition between the Jewish Agency's leader, David Ben-Gurion, and, from 1943, the Irgun's leader, Menachem Begin, both of whom would eventually become prime ministers of Israel.

In 1940, Jabotinsky journeyed to the United States to strengthen Revisionist Zionism there. During his stay, he suffered a heart attack and died. He had brought with him on the trip a significant colleague, Hillel Kook. Born in 1915 in what was then the Russian Empire, Kook came with a pedigree. He was born to the younger brother of Rabbi Abraham Isaac Kook, who served as the first Ashkenazic chief rabbi of the British Mandate. Recognizing ethnic tensions, there were and continue to be two chief rabbis, one for Ashkenazic Jews (that is, generally, those descended from German and European Jews) and one for Sephardic Jews (that is, generally, those descended from Spanish and Middle Eastern Jews). Perhaps in deference to protecting his uncle and the family name or perhaps simply for operational reasons, Kook changed his name to Peter Bergson after he took over the role as head of both the Irgun and the broader Revisionist movement in the United States after Jabotinsky's death.

In July 1944, Bergson created the American League for a Free Palestine (also known as the Bergson Group) with the goal of supporting the Hebrew Committee of National Liberation in Palestine, which provided funds for the broader work of the Irgun in resisting British control and gaining independence.

Bergson was a public relations genius. He considered how he could "sell" the Revisionist philosophy. Many Americans, including many American Jews, did not differentiate between the Haganah and the Irgun. For them, supporting the Jewish people in Palestine was supporting the Jewish people, no matter the group. Bergson's principal technique was to compare the efforts of Jews to establish their own state to the colonists in America trying to form their own independent nation. He would claim, for example, that "it's 1776 in Palestine." Because it might have been difficult to convince Americans that the Irgun members hanged by the British Mandatory Authorities were legitimate fighters, Bergson rebranded these men by comparing them to Nathan Hale. When Bergson organized a boycott of goods produced in the United Kingdom, he compared the effort to the colonists who had boycotted British goods in revolutionary times. On all of the league's press releases, Bergson quoted Thomas Jefferson: "Resistance to tyranny is obedience to God."

The league organized mass demonstrations that deliberately sought to attract audiences by including singers, dancers, and others. Part of Bergson's incredible skill set was to attract the support of famous people who may or may not have understood that they were supporting Irgun specifically and were not supporting the Haganah and the Jewish Agency.

As Dr. Rafael Medoff, the director of the David S. Wyman Institute for Holocaust Studies and the author of *Militant Zionism in America*, puts it, "My sense is that average Jews did not really distinguish between the Haganah and the Irgun and viewed them all as 'the underground' or 'the rebels.'"

Over time, Bergson and the American League for a Free Palestine, through the untiring efforts of Stella Adler, who came from one of the major families in the Yiddish theater and who had introduced the Stanislavsky method of acting in America, recruited a wide variety of supporters. Some gave money. Some gave speeches. Some lent their names to ads. These league supporters included Frank Sinatra; Leonard Bernstein; Milton Berle; Bob Hope; the brilliant singer Paul Robeson; the singers Eddie Cantor and Perry Como; the actors Burgess Meredith, Melvyn Douglas, Vincent Price (who served as chair of the league's annual dinner in Los Angeles), and Sir Cedric Hardwicke; the comedians Carl Reiner, Groucho Marx, Harpo Marx, and Jimmy Durante; the producer David O. Selznick; the director Ernst Lubitsch; the artist Arthur Szyk; Hubert Humphrey, then mayor of Minneapolis and eventually vice president of the United States; and boxing legend Barney Ross.

Adler found a way to convince all these people at a crucial time. Celebrities always draw attention to a cause, but in those days public celebrities were very reluctant to speak about a social or political issue. As Adler later recalled of her efforts for the Irgun, the effort was "one of the most important experiences of my life. The people were men of value, aristocrats of the mind, with social responsibility and the force to do something about it."

In June 1944, the league published a two-page spread boldly proclaiming their message in the influential *New Republic*. Twenty members of Congress were among those who signed the message, as did Stella Adler and another actress, Jane Wyatt.

Many of these celebrities lent their prominent names to the cause. But others went beyond that. Paul O'Dwyer, a lawyer, Irish activist, and brother of the mayor of New York, and Adam Clayton Powell, a prominent African American member of Congress, once worked together to help. They were backstage at a league rally in Madison Square Garden in 1948. A former member of the British army was onstage doing a terrible job of trying to raise funds for the league. Powell became upset at what was happening and whispered to O'Dwyer, "This guy's blowing it, Paul. I think this calls for a Baptist minister and an Irish revolutionary. You handle that microphone over there, and I'll handle this one." They rose together and took the microphones away from the speaker. Also together, they raised $75,000 that evening for the cause.

Donations sometimes came from unexpected sources. Reputed mobster Meyer Lansky sent in a $25,000 contribution.

Mickey Cohen, another gangster, spoke to the league's Ben Hecht (to be discussed below) and offered to host a party to raise funds. The Haganah attempted to convince Cohen that they deserved the money more than the Irgun, but Cohen, suffused with a gangster's code, heard that the Haganah had "squealed" to the British about the Irgun. This deeply displeased Cohen, and he stuck with Hecht. Cohen held his party at Slapsy Maxie's Café in Los Angeles. Hecht recalled speaking to "a thousand bookies, ex-prize fighters, gamblers, jockeys, touts and all sorts of lawless and semi-lawless characters—and their womenfolk." Cohen, not an easy man to please, was not happy with the amount pledged during the initial round. He then ordered his bodyguard to take the stage and demand that the pledges be doubled. "Tell 'em it's for Jews ready to knock hell out of all the bums in the world who don't like them." The bodyguard, not the single most articulate speaker in Hollywood, did his best. Then Cohen stood on the edge of the stage, bathed in floodlights. He didn't speak. One by one, those in attendance stood up and doubled their pledge. The Irgun raised $200,000 that evening.

Cohen also provided his men to guard league meetings. No one would be allowed to stop the Irgun from doing its job.

Barney Ross, who had won lightweight, welterweight, and junior welterweight championships in the 1930s and who later received a war decoration for his efforts at the Battle of Guadalcanal, was another league supporter. Ross, more than anyone, including the gangsters, was the living American symbol of Jewish toughness. Ross spoke at league rallies around the country. During the summer of 1947, he stood on Manhattan's street corners with other league activists and tried to recruit American fighters for a "George Washington Legion" to fight the British in Palestine. Ross no doubt astonished pedestrians as they recognized who was talking to them.

In one of their efforts, the Bergson Group sought to alert Americans to what was happening to the Jews in Europe. On March 9, 1943, Bergson organized *We Will Never Die*, a program offered at Madison Square Garden in New York City. The show later toured various cities in the entire country. The talent gathered for the show was incredible. Billy Rose and Ernst Lubitsch produced the show. Kurt Weill composed the musical score. Moss Hart, then most famous for his collaborations with George S. Kaufman as a playwright, staged the show. It starred Edward G. Robinson, Sylvia Sidney, and Paul Muni.

The show was written by Ben Hecht, who knew exactly what the Irgun was doing and fully supported it.

Hecht was born in New York in 1894. His family moved to Wisconsin, where he grew up. At sixteen, the unhappy Hecht fled to Chicago, where he pursued a career in journalism. He soon began writing novels as well. It was in Chicago that he met Charles Macarthur, another reporter. They moved to New York and collaborated on a play called *The Front Page*, a drama about journalism that gained great fame, especially after multiple film versions.

It was while he was living in New York that the screenwriter Herman J. Mankiewicz sent Hecht a telegram from Hollywood: "Millions are to be grabbed out here and your only competition is idiots. Don't let this get around."

Hecht began by writing the story and screenplay for *Underworld*, the 1927 Josef von Sternberg film. He won the first Academy Award for Best Original Screenplay. He went on to a staggeringly successful career in Hollywood.

Bergson contacted Hecht in September 1941. Up until that meeting, Hecht had no interest in his Jewish heritage. Bergson tried to convince him that people thought of him as Jewish. Hecht insisted that he was simply an American. To test this, Bergson told Hecht to choose three friends and ask them whether he was an American or a Jew. Hecht wrote in his autobiography, *Child of the Century*, that all three of his friends said that he was a Jew.

Hecht and the American League for a Free Palestine collaborated on what was perhaps the league's most noteworthy effort because it created so much publicity and had a surprising ancillary effect on the nation.

This was the play *A Flag Is Born*.

Ben Hecht knew a good story, he knew how to tell it, and from his own writing, in particular for the movies, he was especially adept at stirring emotions. Crucially for the Jews interested in helping Israel, Hecht married his writing talent not only to politics but more specifically to political activism. In the aftermath of the Holocaust, of anti-Semitic outbreaks that broke out even after the war, of the British refusal to let poor survivors living in displaced persons camps immigrate to the Land of Israel, Hecht became determined to present the Zionist case. Unlike scholars or passionate activists lacking dramatic skills, however, Hecht knew precisely how to reach people. His goal was to create images that were both dramatic and simple. As in anthemic songs, the idea was to be comprehended easily by everyone and remembered. Hecht had some clear political goals. He needed a play that made viewers hostile toward the British policies in Palestine and sympathetic to the Jews fighting those policies. This was more difficult than it seemed because in supporting the Irgun over the Haganah, Hecht was actively condoning the killing of British soldiers. Americans might not be in favor of that.

Hecht's genius, though, was his insight, drawn as much from the limitations of his own abilities as from making any intellectual conclusions, that the British were no fascists. They were a civilized people subject to public political pressure. Therefore, the goal for Hecht was a psychological one. He wanted to win over world opinion. He wanted to influence the White House and members of Congress. The fighters in Palestine waged their revolt on one front. Hecht would man the barricades on another. He knew the British had emotional limitations. They had just lost a lot of men against Adolf Hitler and Benito Mussolini. The British public was war weary; they didn't want to have their fathers, sons, and brothers die in the heat of Palestine. Additionally, the British looked terrible in the court of public opinion as they turned away children and adults who had survived Hitler's camps.

Most playwrights want glory and fame, money, and all that emerges from public success. Hecht, however, was a passionate and dedicated Zionist. He wanted money to buy ships to bring Jews home.

In 1946, Hecht wrote a one-act play titled *A Flag Is Born*. The play takes place in a European cemetery. Tevya and Zelda, two elderly and ill Holocaust survivors, are making their arduous journey to the Land of Israel. They stop at the cemetery to rest because it is the eve of the Sabbath. Tevya begins to pray, and as he does so he has a series of strange visions. Jewish sages, kings, and heroes from the past appear in the visions. Hecht's point here is that the Jewish return to their homeland gives rebirth to a nation that they had previously possessed. Their separation from their homeland provides Hecht with a chance to describe not only the Jewish right to the land but also their desperate need for it. Near the end of the play, another character, David, a young man who has survived the Treblinka death camp, comes to the cemetery. He is also on his way to the Land of Israel, where he intends to take up arms and fight the British. Tevya and Zelda die, Hecht's combination of a moving tribute to the Jewish past and a statement of its demise. But David delivers a rousing Zionist speech and as the play ends, goes to fight for Jewish revival. He takes Tevya's prayer shawl and makes a makeshift Zionist flag.

Luther Adler, Stella Adler's brother and one of the great stars of the Yiddish theater, volunteered to direct Hecht's play. Stella chose Celia Adler, their half-sister, to play Zelda and Paul Muni as Tevya.

Muni was then a prominent Hollywood actor. He had starred in one of the earliest gangster movies, *Scarface* (1932). The film was written by Ben Hecht. In that same year, Muni also had starred in *I Am a Fugitive from a Chain Gang*, for which he received an Oscar nomination for Best Actor. He also made an important film of particular Jewish interest: *The Life of Emile Zola* (1937), which focused on the Dreyfus trial and was, intentionally or not, an indictment of what was then occurring in Nazi Germany.

Kurt Weill created an original score for the play. Quentin Reynolds, whose voice was then well known as a journalist who had covered important World War II battles, served as the narrator. The role of David was pivotal, for he had to be young and forceful. Dramatically, he represented the future. Hecht conferred with the Adlers. Stella recommended her most promising drama pupil. He was twenty-two and not Jewish.

His name was Marlon Brando. As he later wrote, Brando was interested in the part because of "what we were beginning to learn about the true nature of the killing of the Jews and because of the empathy I felt for the Adlers and the other Jews who had become my friends and teachers and who told me of their dreams for a Jewish State." Of course, Brando was much more an actor than a Zionist. He relished the opportunity to work with Paul Muni. Brando recalled that for him, Muni was "the only actor who ever moved me to leave my dressing room to watch him from the wings."

Brando, as did all the actors, worked for minimum wage according to the guidelines from the guild for actors. (Brando's appearance in *A Flag Is Born* was not his only effort on behalf of the league. The league later produced *Last Night We Attacked*, a brief film about Jewish fighters who fought the British. Brando served as a guest speaker for showings of the film around the country.)

Rehearsals began in a studio above Al & Dick's Restaurant, which was located on West Fifty-Fourth Street in New York City. Muni was a perfectionist. He wanted the work done his way and was especially tough on the young Brando. Perhaps Brando's good looks, his toughness, his acting skills, and the fact that he had so much more of his life ahead of him than Muni did made Muni jealous. Muni was no Method actor. He didn't like words spoken slowly to emphasize emotions. He wanted to move the action along, and so he was infuriated that Brando spoke so slowly, once complaining about Brando, "You can drive trucks through the spaces in his cues." Muni then walked off the set. He was also displeased over a part of the script that required Brando's character to go over to the dead Tevya, Muni's character, and cover his face with a prayer shawl. Muni was not an actor who ever wanted his face covered. He told Brando not to do it. Brando did as he was asked in rehearsals, but on opening night Brando stuck with Hecht's script and covered Muni's face. Brando tried to do it again on the second night, but this time the dead Tevya slowly began pulling the shawl down so that the audience could see Muni's face in all its glory.

Brando stayed at Hecht's home in Nyack, north of New York, between rehearsals. It was here that Brando ran across a wide variety of people, including celebrities, who supported the Zionist cause. As Hecht recalled, "Around me in Nyack the Palestinian underground crackled constantly. Russian and British spies pattered through the house and eavesdropped at the swimming pool where the Irgun captains were wont to gather for disputation." Hecht noted that Brando and others there "eased the political tensions of the household" by playing a celebrity baseball game in the rain.

The play opened on September 5, 1946. Almost immediately, the play, as it was meant to do, stirred emotions deeply. Everyone knew Paul Muni was a brilliant actor. But the audience wasn't familiar with the power of Marlon Brando. Perhaps Brando's most confrontational speech in the play involved a dramatic statement about what American

Jews had done and not done about Hitler. Brando, playing David, delivers a speech that was pure Ben Hecht. In the play, the character loudly and fiercely criticized American Jews for not confronting President Franklin D. Roosevelt, for letting him get away with not saving more Jews and not helping Jewish refugees. As David, Brando cried out, "Where were you, Jews? Where were you when six million Jews were being burned to death in the ovens? Where were you?" Brando, the consummate actor, delivered these lines by starting quietly and growing louder as he repeated his accusatory question. Brando recalled that at some performances, some young Jewish women stood in the aisles screaming and crying.

The play provoked intense passions. Emotionally, it was a call to overcome guilt about being silent while six million Jews died in the Holocaust. There was a theme of death and redemption. The new Jewish nation would be the redemption, a chance to overcome the grief and horror and guilt so many American Jews felt.

After the opening night performance, Ben Hecht came out onstage. He asked the audience for donations: "Give us your money, and we will turn it into history."

The audience responded. It is unclear whether the audience was made up exclusively or even primarily of Jews. As Rafael Medoff suggested in a private e-mail to the author of this book: "There is no way to know who attended *A Flag Is Born*. They were not necessarily attending in order to support Hecht or the Irgun or anything else." This is an important point. Once the play became successful and well reviewed, people attended because of the success and reviews. They may not have even been aware of the content, much less supportive of the general views of Hecht. That, in fact, may have been a key to the play's success. It attracted such a large audience and, given Hecht's writing skills and the incredible acting, especially of Muni and Brando, people who had no knowledge of or interest in the plight of the Jews suddenly got caught up in the emotions Hecht so brilliantly offered.

The original intention was to run *A Flag Is Born* for a month in the Alvin Theater on Broadway and Fifty-Second Street and then to take it on tour. However, the reaction to the play was overwhelming. The play eventually ran for 120 performances stretching over two and a half months. As Dr. Rafael Medoff wrote:

> The response that "Flag" evoked was due in part to the public's sympathy for the victims of Nazi genocide and the Holocaust survivors languishing in European Displaced Persons camps. But that was not the only reason. The Bergson group's public information efforts cleverly emphasized symbols, images, and phrases comparing the Jewish fighters in Palestine to the heroes of the American Revolution.

In advertisements and press releases, the Irgun said England had a policy of "taxation without representation."

The committee supporting *A Flag Is Born* recruited the likes of Eleanor Roosevelt, then still very famous as the former first lady of the United States; Leonard Bernstein, the composer; and the then prominent novelist Lion Feuchtwanger.

It might be assumed that the entire Jewish community welcomed the support of these and other prominent and celebrated people. But even after the Holocaust, there were still Jews who opposed the creation of a Jewish nation. Judah Magnes, who served as president of the Hebrew University of Jerusalem, was so opposed to the idea of a particularly Jewish state that he wrote an open letter to Eleanor Roosevelt that was published in the *New York Times*. Denouncing Hecht's play, Magnes argued that it encouraged violence. Magnes wanted Roosevelt to withdraw her support of the play, although she did not do so.

Perhaps the most interesting review of the play came from the *Hollywood Reporter*. The publication's reviewer wrote: "Reviewing is costing us money. Ben Hecht has written so moving a pageant in *A Flag Is Born* that we have been moved to pen not only a congratulatory critique—but to write a check to the American League for a Free Palestine in its repatriation program." The *New Yorker* had among the most critical of reviews, calling the play "a combination of dubious poetry and political oversimplification."

When the Broadway run was completed, *A Flag Is Born* began performances in various cities. Brando, the only Gentile in the play, was so committed to the part that he supposedly turned down the opportunity to star in a forthcoming film about anti-Semitism, *Gentleman's Agreement*. (The part went eventually to Gregory Peck, and the film became very influential.) Brando explained his reason for staying with the play: "I want to keep doing what I'm doing. These people are persecuted, and they need help."

Hecht and Bergson took the play to Detroit, Philadelphia, Baltimore, Chicago, and Boston. In various places, Luther Adler replaced Paul Muni and Stella Adler took over the narration. The tour took six months, but so famous had it become that *A Flag Is Born* then toured South America. It also had an unusual performance. The play, translated into Hebrew, was performed in Cyprus in a British detention camp. Of course, the British banned the play in the United Kingdom and all the lands it controlled, including Palestine.

The play had several purposes. Its organizers wanted to provide information to the Jewish and general community. They wanted to stir America to push Britain at the very moment that Britain was deciding what to do about Palestine. And, crucially, they wanted the play to serve as a mechanism to raise funds. In fact, the combined total of revenues from ticket sales and donations made after performances likely reached close to $1 million. Additionally, in October 1946 there was a dinner held to honor Paul Muni, and $74,000 was raised at that dinner. Part of these funds was used to purchase a ship to bring Holocaust survivors to the Land of Israel. (The story of this ship will be told in the next chapter.)

Rafael Medoff assesses the play's most crucial impact:

> Perhaps most importantly, *Flag* contributed to the process of persuading the British to withdraw from Palestine. Reports from British diplomats in the United States back to their superiors in London bemoaned *Flag*'s effectiveness in turning American public opinion against England. This came at a time when the British government was anxious for U.S. support, including the provision of desperately-

needed postwar loans for economic reconstruction. The damage that *Flag* and similar activities inflicted on England's image abroad, coming on top of the casualties inflicted on British forces in Palestine by the Jewish underground fighters, played a role in the process that brought about London's decision to withdraw from the Holy Land, paving the way for the creation of the State of Israel.

A Flag Is Born was intended to focus on a specific matter: the struggle for an independent Jewish nation in the Land of Israel. Sometimes, however, there are unintended consequences of actions.

In the case of *A Flag Is Born*, that unintended consequence involved race relations in the United States at the time. The play was scheduled to play at the National Theater in Washington, DC. The theater was privately owned. Some private theaters refused to admit black patrons. Others let blacks into the performances but confined them to the balcony. In being seated separately, the black audiences were forced to confront their inferior status in a humiliating way. They were, at least passively, forced to accept the system of segregation. The National Theater was among those that completely barred black patrons.

This discrimination against blacks was repulsive to many dramatists. In November 1946, thirty-three important playwrights, including Irving Berlin and Oscar Hammerstein, announced that they would not allow their plays to be performed at any theater in Washington that discriminated against black patrons. That ban included the National Theater.

Ben Hecht was among those who signed the statement. *A Flag Is Born* was withdrawn from the National and rescheduled for a performance in a Baltimore theater, the Maryland. A special train car was arranged to transport the members of Congress, including eighteen U.S. senators, who had planned to attend the Washington performance to Baltimore instead.

This bold attempt to combat blatant racism no doubt sounded like a good idea. However, a problem immediately arose. Unknown to the league, the Maryland Theater didn't bar black patrons completely, but it was among the theaters that restricted them to the balcony.

A plan was hatched. Several hours before the play was about to begin, a league representative went to the manager of the Maryland Theater with a clear warning: if the theater did not end the way it discriminated against blacks, there would be an NAACP (National Association for the Advancement of Colored People) picket line, and those picketing would not be happy. By coincidence, the performance was scheduled for February 12, Abraham Lincoln's birthday. The theater manager was reminded of this, and so the manager was alerted to the potential news value of a protest about prejudice against blacks on the very day celebrating the president who issued the Emancipation Proclamation.

The pressure worked. All of a sudden, the league, as the legal lessee, found itself in charge of the seating arrangements. There were at least ten blacks who attended the performance. They were not restricted to the balcony. There were no protests outside or among the audience.

Hecht said after the first performance in Baltimore: "I am proud that it was my play which terminated one of the most disgraceful practices of our country's history."

Leaders of the NAACP used this incredible victory to end discrimination in other Baltimore theaters, the first time in the history of the state of Maryland that African Americans were permitted to attend the legitimate theater without discrimination. Hecht wrote,

> I am proud that it was *A Flag Is Born* which they attended without insult. Breaking down this vicious and indecent tradition in Maryland is worthy of the high purpose for which *Flag* was conceived and written. The incident is forceful testimony to the proposition that to fight discrimination and injustice to one group of human beings affords protection to every other group.

The efforts of the Irgun in America were moderately successful. In some ways, their greatest triumph was stirring public opinion and in getting Americans, including American Jews, to be reluctant or unable to distinguish between the Haganah and the Irgun. In the Land of Israel, the Haganah was so wholly dissatisfied with the violence of the

Irgun (and its more violent offshoot, the Sternists, named after their founder, Avraham Stern) that the Haganah tried to end the existence of the other groups. For a while, it appeared as though there would be a Jewish civil war. The League for a Free Palestine reacted by calling the Haganah traitors for not attacking British soldiers and forcing the British to leave the land.

In 1946, the Irgun bombed the King David Hotel, which served as British military headquarters, and killed ninety-one people. The league strongly praised this action and considered British retaliation to be mimicking Hitler.

Ben Hecht, in response to what was happening in Palestine, wrote an open letter to what he intended as an ironically named audience: the "Terrorists of Palestine." The May 15, 1947, letter read as follows:

> My Brave Friends . . . .
> The Jews of America are for you. You are their champions. You are the grin that they wear. You are the feather in their hats.
> In the past fifteen hundred years every nation of Europe has taken a crack at the Jews. This time the British are at bat. You are the first answer that makes sense—to the New World.
> Every time you blow up a British arsenal, or wreck a British jail, or send a British train sky high, or rob a British bank or let go with your guns and bombs at the British betrayers and invaders of your homeland, the Jews of America make a little holiday in their hearts.

The real struggle in the Land of Israel, the dirty, bloody battles between the Jews and the Arabs, the Jews and the British, and the Jews and the Jews, were mostly not understood in America. For many Americans, the simple emotional and financial support they gave was meant to be given to some abstract idea of Jewish fighters struggling for a free land after the Holocaust, not to a specific political group.

This broad understanding helped the Irgun, which didn't have to explain its fights with the Haganah. And it helped the Haganah because increased public pressure was brought on the British.

Both the Haganah and the Irgun also fought the British in another way. Beyond raising money and obtaining arms, the Haganah (and to a lesser extent the Irgun) obtained ships to break the British blockade and bring the remnants of European Jewry who sought refuge in their ancient homeland to the shores of the Land of Israel.

And Americans were there to help them in this effort.

6

FROM SURVIVORS TO IMMIGRANTS

The British had carried through on their determined effort to keep the Jewish refugees, often the broken and bent survivors of the death camps and the ghettos, of the forests and the attics where they had hidden, from reaching their Promised Land. In 1945, about one hundred thousand Jewish survivors were traveling through Europe, seeking a way to get to Palestine. Despite the emerging news of the Holocaust, news that numbed and then shocked the world, that year the British allowed only 13,100 Jews to enter Palestine. Shockingly, fifteen hundred fewer Jews entered Palestine that year than the year before. As the need became greater, as the opportunity for Jews to escape increased for however narrow a time frame, the British tightened their border controls.

But the Jews in the Land of Israel, the Jews in Europe, and some Jews in the United States could not accept the situation. They were determined. And so in the United States, Americans, Haganah leaders, and, separately, Irgun leaders decided there was only one course open. They would obtain boats in America, recruit American volunteers, pick up the refugees, and smash through the British blockade. There was a determination to bring the survivors to their traditional homeland.

At the end of the British Mandate and just before the formal birth of Israel, thirty-two thousand refugees, about half the number of all the refugees who came from Europe during this time period, came on American vessels.

The coordinated effort began after the British rejected a May 1, 1946, recommendation by the Anglo-American Commission to admit one hundred thousand refugees to Palestine. Furious, Ben-Gurion determined that the Jews would bring in ten thousand refugees a month, by stealth if necessary. As he had made clear at the founding meeting of the Sonneborn Institute, Ben-Gurion needed the refugees, and they needed him. They faced physical danger, starvation, abuse, and rejection where they were. Ben-Gurion needed them to fight, and he needed them for another type of war, one hidden from public view. This was the demographic war. How many Jews and how many Arabs lived in Palestine? Where did they live? Ben-Gurion was aware that any division of the land would be into areas with a Jewish majority and an Arab majority. And so both sides played a sort of demographic roulette, seeking to maximize their population and its location.

As noted in chapter 3, Ben-Gurion sent Danny Shind to the United States to organize this effort. The effort was given the overall name of Aliyah Bet. Bet is the second letter of the Hebrew alphabet, and aliyah means immigrating to Israel. The primary means of aliyah was legal, but especially in the years between the end of the Second World War in Europe in 1945 and the establishment of Israel in 1948, because of British policy, the emphasis for Jews had to be on the coordinated movements of Aliyah Bet to bring Jews to Palestine.

Two Canadian corvettes, the *Wedgwood* and the *Haganah*, were the first ships to transport refugees. (The word *ship* is used loosely in the book. Technically, a ship operates in deep water. A boat is nautically smaller than a ship and indeed can be carried on a ship. The word *ship* is therefore used in a nontechnical way here.) There had been an Aliyah Bet effort as the war progressed, but that effort naturally took on an entirely different character after the war. In the middle of 1946, these two ships carried about five thousand refugees over the course of a single month. That number almost equaled the entire Aliyah Bet effort up until that point.

It was the third ship, the *Haim Arlosoroff*, that began the more violent and vicious phase of the Aliyah Bet efforts. The ship was named for the head of the political department of the Jewish Agency. The British fired on the *Arlosoroff* with machine guns, but the immigrant-filled ship evaded the British attempt to board it and send its passengers to a displaced persons camp in Cyprus. The ship reached the Haifa area. This literal opening shot in the ongoing battle to bring new immigrants to the Land of Israel would dramatically escalate with further ships.

The story of these immigrant ships began in the United States with the obtaining of vessels. This effort was not part of a clandestine program, but rather it was done in full compliance with American law. The ships were purchased, refitted, equipped, and then registered under the flags of Panama or Honduras. Flying those flags, the ships then traveled to Europe. Indeed, no American was ever prosecuted for helping Jewish refugees return to their ancient homeland. Of course, part of the task involved recruiting volunteers to work on the ships.

Danny Shind's dedication was a key component of the effort. Joe Buxenbaum, who had served in the U.S. Army during World War II, was recruited as an aide by Shind. The two were the overall inspectors. They found many of the ships. They inspected the vessels to determine whether they were seaworthy. When necessary, the ships were refitted under their direction. They also went to the docks as the ships were preparing to sail.

As a Palestinian Jew, Shind was forbidden from buying any ships himself. He needed someone who could fulfill that function and found that someone in Morris Ginsberg. Ginsberg, of the American Foreign Steamship Corporation, came from a family deeply involved in the shipping business. He was the one who had invaluable connections in that business. It was Ginsberg, working on behalf of the Aliyah Bet operation in America, who acquired the two Royal Canadian Navy corvettes that soon were renamed the *Wedgwood* and the *Haganah*, which were the first two Aliyah Bet ships that American crews ran. Ginsberg's connection to the operation was so close that he eventually married Danny Shind's secretary.

William C. Ash was another important person in the Aliyah Bet American effort. A U.S. Maritime Service officer during the Second World War, Ash, who had been born in Poland, had served as a port captain for Ginsberg's corporation. He eventually established a business as a marine surveyor.

One day, the Jewish Agency called Ash and asked for a meeting. Shind bluntly and directly described Aliyah Bet activities to Ash at the meeting, but the hard-bitten Ash refused to get involved in any illegal activities. However, he wondered aloud, why didn't Aliyah Bet simply conduct their activities in a legal manner? Ash explained that all the activities Shind described could be accomplished legally. He explained that, after all, American shipowners frequently organized dummy companies in a foreign land and then got a foreign flag of convenience. Such a foreign company could be created, Ash explained, for the relatively low sum of $500.

Shind was captivated by the idea, no doubt less concerned by the legality of what he thought to be a cause of the highest moral value than by the realization that he could attract people like William Ash, who might otherwise be resistant to joining the effort. And so Shind established Arias and Arias, a Panamanian company that was in fact no more than a paper company with a proper mailing address. The Weston Trading Company, a new American corporation, was also established.

Dewey Stone, a friend of Chaim Weizmann, was the only stockholder in the Weston Trading Company. Because Stone was a well-known philanthropist, he could write large checks without anyone becoming suspicious. Indeed, on one occasion the Federal Bureau of Investigation came to question Stone about his efforts. He simply said the ship in question was being prepared to send clothing to refugees in Europe. Stone's very real business ventures made such a response plausible and ended the investigation.

Ash, who also served as an official in the Masters, Mates, and Pilots Union, was perfectly positioned to identify potential sailors.

The Palestine Vocational Service was yet another front corporation set up with the express purpose of recruiting volunteers to serve on the Aliyah Bet ships. Ralph Goldman was the director of the service.

The volunteers who served did not receive any pay. They got small sums for various needs, and they had to agree to obey the Haganah's rules. Indeed, prior to sailing overseas, the volunteers were sworn in as Haganah members. These sailors, Jewish and Gentile, coming from all parts of American life, were far from typical crews.

I. F. Stone, who would later achieve considerable fame for his muckraking journalistic style of carefully scrutinizing official documents and uncovering facts that others had missed, was onboard the first two Aliyah Bet ships and, careful observer that he was, recorded his experiences. His journeys were described in his book *Underground to Palestine*. What makes his analysis particularly interesting is that he and some of the people he described were on the political left in American politics, in some cases on the extreme left. It is worth noting since in the current political climate in America, much of the fiercest political support for Israel comes from the Orthodox and the politically conservative. There was a time, as Stone notes, when Zionism was an attractive cause for the Left, so attractive that, like fighting in Spain's civil war and other ventures, volunteers from the Left were willing to put their lives on the line for a Jewish state. Stone's precise prose provides revealing portraits of the wide variety of people who made up the crews that sailed the ships. For example, Stone said the *Wedgwood* was "manned by about as odd a collection of seamen as ever sailed the sea." Stone wrote about the captain and the first mate, who were both former members of the Industrial Workers of the World, a far-left organization:

> Like many of the sailors I was to meet on these illegal ships, neither of these officers was Jewish by anything but an accident of birth. They had little Jewish upbringing and no Jewish education, and were, of course, not at all religious. But they had left families in America and taken the risk of long sentences in British prisons if caught. The said they were "sore as a —— boil" about the treatment

the Jews had received in Europe. They spoke a thick Brooklynese, heavily seasoned with favorite GI expletives.

These officers were matched by ordinary members of the crew. Stone related his view of the crew on the *Haganah* this way:

> Many of the crew members were New Yorkers. Others came from Chicago, Los Angeles, Baltimore, Washington, Boston, Jersey City, and New Haven. There was a Canadian boy from Toronto. Only one chief engineer was non-Jewish.
>
> Most of the crew had served in the Army, Navy, or Merchant Marine during the war. Some joined the crew because they were Zionists. A lot of them were American Chalutzim [pioneers] who intended to remain in the collective settlements in Palestine.
>
> The rest were simply American sailors who happened to be Jews, boys with little if any past contact with Jewish life. They spoke neither Yiddish nor Hebrew. They were not very articulate, but for them the trip was more than a heroic adventure. They all felt deeply about the treatment of Jews in Europe, and this was their way of doing something about it.

Other volunteers from all over the country signed up. Many had the same motivations as discussed by I. F. Stone, but others had personal motivations or were influenced by history and reading. There were, for example, two prominent books, both written by Gentile authors, that challenged British policies in the Middle East. *Behind the Silken Curtain* by Bartley C. Crum and *The Forgotten Ally* by Pierre Van Paassen both motivated Jewish readers to volunteer in efforts to bring Jewish immigrants to Palestine. Reading became a great motivator because it provided basic information and emotional context, and offered a gateway to use the information and emotions aroused by the books. There were many examples of reading being the decisive factor in recruitment. A rabbi's son at Harvard Law School, a former naval officer, read I. F. Stone's book and together with a classmate who was an Irish Gentile joined the Aliyah Bet effort.

With the recruitment efforts going well, the fundamental task of acquiring ships continued. After Morris Ginsberg's acquisition of the corvettes, the Weston Trading Company purchased the *Unalga*, a former coast guard cutter. The ship got a flag from Honduras and, renamed the *Ulna* (after a river in Honduras), the ship was renamed again as the *Haim Arlosoroff*.

The attempt to rescue refugees was of such overriding humanitarian importance that it became the effort that brought the Haganah and the Irgun together. The Irgun asked Morris Ginsberg to help in refitting a ship. Ginsberg, who must have been baffled by the politics involved, asked Danny Shind what to do, and Shind told him to cooperate. In Europe, the Haganah's Aliyah Bet workers cooperated with the Irgun in helping refugees get on a ship run by the Irgun. Indeed, the ship, a four-hundred-ton vessel that had previously been a yacht known as the S.S. *Abril*, was renamed in honor of Ben Hecht.

Paul Shulman was another important worker for Aliyah Bet. Shulman, who had graduated from Annapolis and served in the United States Navy, was from a prominent American Zionist family. Shulman met Shlomo Rabinovich one day and asked about the plans that were being made for a navy in the new Jewish nation. Rabinovich was astounded by the idea and thought it beyond any current efforts. He sent Shulman to an office to help with Aliyah Bet. (After sailing on some of the Aliyah Bet ships, Paul Shulman would eventually become the first chief of staff of the Israeli Navy and its second commander.) Shulman began his work for Aliyah Bet by purchasing two ships.

Samuel Zemurray (whose widely used nickname was Sam the Banana Man) was another important American who helped with Aliyah Bet efforts. Zemurray was an immigrant who, at age twenty, began peddling bananas in Alabama. He quickly acquired some money. Zemurray was eventually the owner of the United Fruit Company, which, among other holdings, controlled factories in Honduras. When Aliyah Bet was trying to acquire some vessels, Shind traveled to Louisiana to talk to Zemurray and got the vessels from Zemurray's company, but the travel was a courtesy visit to be honest with Zemurray, a friend of Chaim

Weizmann, and tell him that the ships would be used for Aliyah Bet. There are various stories about what happened next. One of the stories, a tale that added to Zemurray's later famous Zionist legend, was that Shind was having trouble getting a flag and papers from a Latin American nation. According to this story, Zemurray called the head of the country, who was a general, and casually informed the ruler that the cost of bananas that Zemurray bought had fallen. Zemurray pointed out that this decline in cost meant he would offset his losses by paying a lower cost for the bananas he got from that country. He explained that the decline in cost came from the fact that a ship he needed was delayed from sailing because it couldn't sail under the country's flag and lacked papers. The general quickly replied that he could arrange for the necessary flag and papers. In that case, Zemurray said, the price of bananas had risen back to its original level.

Most of the ships that eventually sailed were from the Haganah, but, as mentioned earlier, the Irgun also participated. Their effort started in October 1946, a few weeks after the play *A Flag Is Born* opened. The American League for a Free Palestine held a testimonial dinner for Paul Muni and announced that the $74,000 raised would be used to buy ships to break the British blockade and bring displaced Jews back to their ancient homeland. Muni concluded his own speech at the dinner by quoting some of his lines in the play:

> Remember, Englishmen, that you have never won a war against a people that wanted to be free! So why make such another war and lose it? And lose your own honor, also. Lose all the fine things that Englishmen fought for—when they were defending themselves—and called the world to help them by crying that everybody should be allowed to live on earth without fear of oppression. . . .
>
> Listen to me, Americans. My people were killed in Europe by the Germans. . . . Let them into Palestine or they die—all that are left. Why did you fight the Germans, so you could take over their work of killing the rest of the Jews? . . . How many conferences do you need to hold before one of the Freedoms, for which your soldiers fought and died, can exist? . . . Open one little door to Palestine.

Meanwhile, the league established the Tyre Shipping Company, and this company purchased a four-hundred-ton former yacht, the *Cytheria*. Through the summer and fall of 1946, the ship obtained the necessary repairs and loaded provisions for the voyage. The costs for all this might have been beyond the means of the league, except for the fact that they received great help from Morris Ginsberg of the American Foreign Steamship Corporation. Ginsberg had gone to Danny Shind to get permission to cooperate with the Irgun.

A crew was assembled. The ship was registered in Honduras, so the crew needed Honduran seamen's papers. The ship was moved to Staten Island and took on more provisions: a ton of salami, many thousands of vitamin pills, and an abundant supply of canned grapefruit juice.

The *Cytheria* was renamed the S.S. *Abril*, and the ship set sail on December 27, 1946. The ship was manned by a twenty-one-member crew, most of whom were American. Indeed, seven of the crew were from Brooklyn. The ship reached Port de Bouc in France, and it was there that the vessel received its new name, the S.S. *Ben Hecht*. Six hundred survivors of the Holocaust boarded the ship on February 28 and March 1. Again, there was uncharacteristic cooperation between the Haganah and the Irgun that hinted at the eventual cooperation that would occur once the State of Israel was declared. The ship set sail on March 1. There were problems from the beginning of the voyage. The ship had two diesel engines, and one of them was virtually inoperable for most of the voyage. There were two main tanks containing fresh water. One of them leaked almost its entire contents. There were three consecutive days during which the weather made the voyage so turbulent that passengers got ill. On top of that, the underground radio in the Land of Israel that was to guide them never replied to their increasingly frantic signals.

On March 8, 1947, a British ship intercepted the *Ben Hecht* 10.6 miles from the shores of its destination in the Land of Israel. British marines boarded, and the *Ben Hecht* was towed to Haifa. The *Palestine Post* noted:

The vessel had no banners, no Hebrew name. When it was caught, the Honduras flag under which it sailed was brought down and the Jewish colors ran up the mast.

Twenty men, said to be Americans, and suspected of being the crew, were arrested and are being held under strong guard in the Haifa lock-up.

The refugees were put on British vessels and sent to Cyprus to a detention camp.

Meanwhile, the League for a Free Palestine decided that once again they would take a different approach than the Haganah. In a situation in which crew members associated with the Haganah were returned to the United States, Haganah crews assumed false names, hid from the authorities, and tried to hide any association they had with Aliyah Bet activities. In contrast, the league contacted officials of the American consulate to determine the legal status of the crew. The league put out an announcement on March 11 indicating that enough volunteers had come forth in response to the *Ben Hecht* seizure to man five more ships.

One member of the crew disguised himself as a passenger and went to Cyprus along with the genuine passengers. The other members of the crew stayed in jail in Haifa for two days and then were sent to the prison at Acre. There they were tried for aiding and abetting immigration that was illegal. They were found guilty and were sentenced to prison terms of seventeen years.

The Irgun were nothing if not daring. One of the crew members of the *Ben Hecht* carried a camera with him. While he was at Acre prison, he began to take photographs of all the prisoners who would take part in a great escape. The Irgun passed on the film, and the photographs were used as part of the false documents they created. There was a prison breakout on May 4. As the escapees left the prison, they met up with an Irgun representative who gave each of them the false documents.

By then, the volunteer crew on the *Ben Hecht* had already been returned to the United States. Because of the boarding of the ship, the tragic context of the passengers, and the international pressure put on the British, on March 30 the British deported the American volunteers back to the United States. The crew reached New York on April 16.

The attorney general of the United States quickly announced that he would not bring any charges against the crew members. The British were fearful of a fight with the pro-Zionist U.S. Congress about American citizens being imprisoned. The Americans, in the middle of a presidential election, were not about to prosecute the group of young men widely considered as heroic not just by Jewish voters but increasingly by a large number of non-Jewish Americans as well.

Two days after the crew made its way back home, Acting Mayor Vincent R. Impellitteri welcomed them at City Hall in New York and said, "As a war veteran myself, I can understand how you, war veterans, volunteered for this hazardous voyage with no reward for yourselves except the satisfaction of helping to attain American war aims including justice and freedom for all deserving peoples."

The league set up a series of public rallies for the deserving crew and a dinner at Hotel Astor. Ben Hecht was there, as were Milton Berle and Rosalind Russell.

The non-Irgun ships were more plentiful. For example, I. F. Stone was on hand to record the *Haganah*'s first voyage:

> We saw a line of ten trucks heading for the freight terminal. They were open trucks jammed tight with refugees. . . . Crew members waved from the deck and shouted *Shalom*.
>
> Every section of the ship in which there was emergency sleeping space had been given a letter of the alphabet, and every bunk a number. One member of the crew was assigned to each section and instructed to act as usher for the refugees.
>
> On the pier each refugee was given a slip of paper with the letter of his section and the number of his bunk. . . .
>
> The embarkation was complicated by the fact that it had to take place on a Saturday morning, and many of the passengers were Orthodox Jews. One of the underground workers said there had been considerable discussion as to whether it was permissible for such a purpose to travel and to carry bags on the Sabbath. . . .

The majority decided that it was . . . a pious deed for a Jew to go to Palestine and they would therefore be forgiven for what would ordinarily be a sin. But two members . . . stayed behind. They felt that even for such a purpose it was not proper to violate the Sabbath and that they would rather take their chances and wait for another ship. . . .

Among our refugees were five Gentiles who intended to settle in Palestine, four for religious, one for idealistic reasons.

Two thirds of the refugees were men. . . . Most our passengers were 30 years of age or younger. . . . Our oldest passenger was 78; our youngest, 10. . . .

There were Jews from 16 different countries on board. . . . Linguistically, the ship was a floating Babel.

The trip normally should have taken four days. Instead it took twelve days. The refugees lived under terrible conditions during the voyage. They had little ventilation. It was very crowded. They lived in constant anxiety about the threat of British discovery of the ship. At eleven each evening, a curfew began and they had to go below decks, with air that didn't circulate, until daylight. On deck during the day, they swapped stories (except for the lone Egyptian Jew who only spoke Arabic), sang or listened or others, or simply enjoyed the comforting rays of the sun.

Sometimes there were surprise reunions. On the second day of the voyage, a twenty-year-old woman named Ruth was talking with the Americans when she saw a large man about three times her age. She ran over and grabbed him. They had both been in Auschwitz, and he had saved her from execution. They had been separated and hadn't seen each other since then.

Rudy, the man who had saved her, had led a remarkable life. He had grown up in Poland but became an orphan at age eight. Then he had gone to Cuba and engaged in rum running, which led to a term in a U.S. federal penitentiary. Once out, he turned to professional wrestling and joined the circus as a strongman. He had been on a circus tour in Europe in 1939. The outbreak of World War II prevented him from leaving Poland. He was sent to Auschwitz. There, because of his sheer size, he was made a head capo, but he used this position to bribe guards. He set up a black market using gold and jewels from victims who had been sent to the gas chambers and cigarettes, brandy, and meat stolen from storerooms. He used these valuables to buy the lives of Jews, including Ruth, who was scheduled to be hanged the following day when Rudy saw her. He later said, "When I first set eyes on her I loved her as if she were my own daughter. She was such a sweet child. I couldn't let her go to her death. I had to find some way to save her." Rudy then went to the SS officer in charge. The officer was a "client" of Rudy's who received some of his bribes. Rudy brought along a bottle of schnapps, and the two drank. Rudy said, "I can't live without her." And then Rudy promised he would provide jewelry for the officer's mistress, to keep her happy. The officer shouted, "You're a crazy Jew." Rudy got a false death certificate and phony Aryan papers for Ruth, who was sent to a labor camp for Polish women. Rudy continued his work and became famous for saving lives in Auschwitz. He achieved heroic status among the prisoners.

At sunset on the seventh day of the *Haganah*'s voyage, the passengers welcomed the arrival of the Sabbath. But the moments of joy were balanced by the difficulties of the voyage. The Aliyah Bet leadership was concerned because the *Wedgwood*, the other Canadian corvette, had been captured by the British, and they didn't want to lose both ships. A plan was devised to move the passengers onto the Turkish ship *Akbel II*. Since the *Akbel II* was less than half the size of the *Haganah*, passengers were worried about their lives on the new ship. Jamming thirty passengers at a time into motor launches that went from the *Haganah* to the *Akbel*, the passengers began to be transferred. Suddenly, as the last of the belongings were transferred, a British warship was sighted.

The *Akbel* raised a Star of David flag, was renamed the *Biryah* after a Jewish community the British had seized, and started at its very slow maximum speed. The ship had too many passengers and began to list. Concerned about everyone's safety and fearing the ship would capsize, the commander ordered that the radio operator send an SOS. After an intense game of cat and mouse with the British and difficult times among the passengers, the ship was off the Haifa coast, ready to enter the Land of Israel. But British ships were waiting in Haifa's port. A British destroyer escorted the Jews into Haifa's harbor. There, accompanied by Palestinian Arab police, the British took control. The refugees were sent to a detention camp and, according to the quota system the British had imposed, those detained were eventually set free.

The stories of all these ships need a separate volume, and indeed such a volume has been cowritten by one of the heroes who volunteered as an unpaid crew member. The stories of all the voyages can be found in *The Jews' Secret Fleet: The Untold Story of North American Volunteers Who Smashed the British Blockade of Palestine*. The book is written by that hero, Murray S. Greenfield, along with Joseph M. Hochstein. Greenfield sailed on the *Hatikvah*. The story of that voyage is also told in the excellent film *Waves of Freedom*.

This book will limit its stories to two additional ships, the *Hatikvah* and a ship that became world famous, the *Exodus*.

Beyond confronting the British blockade by seeking to bypass it with refugee ships, the Haganah decided to confront the blockade directly with the ship *Hatikvah*.

The voyage of the *Hatikvah* began in February 1947. Once named the *Gresham* and then renamed *Tradewinds*, the ship was built by the Canadians to break the ice on the St. Lawrence River. During the war, the ship served as a coast guard cutter on the Atlantic coast, searching for probing German submarines.

In 1947, the *Tradewinds* was set to go across the Atlantic to bring the refugees to their new home. The Gentile captain of the ship and the crew, some of whom were wholly unprepared for their task and dubious about the condition of the ship, set sail from Miami. After difficulties, the ship made it to Baltimore and gained new volunteers along with additional provisions for the voyage.

A clash of styles emerged on the voyage. The American volunteers were grounded in a specifically American toughness, an irreverent and harsh wit that mocked even the most sacred subjects. But other volunteers were young idealists who had dedicated themselves to the Zionist cause, who had grown up in one or another of the various Zionist youth groups, and who took the cause they had pledged their lives to as very serious, not at all a subject to be made fun of or mocked. Their ideological rigidity offended the tough volunteers, who played tricks on them. They pretended they would take off the forecastle head of the ship and sell it for a profit. This task, which could not be accomplished, so offended the young Zionists that they reported the fictional plot. The idealists wanted the ship run according to democratic rule. The professional sailors had spent their lives learning that the crew followed the orders of a captain and the officers on board.

In a crucial way, the relationship between the Americans and the ardent Zionists is a perfect foreshadowing of the relationship between American Jews and Israeli Jews in that the two had very different perspectives even while both supported the birth and then security of the Jewish state. In some ways, at some later times, Israeli Jews were the flippant ones (for example, mocking national heroes such as Moshe Dayan on television and thereby offending many American Jews who looked upon such iconic figures as heroes). At other times, as in the case of the *Hatikvah*, the reverse was true. George Bernard Shaw once commented that "England and America are two countries separated by a common language." So too are American Jews and Israeli Jews two peoples separated by a common identity and religion. As noted, this separation began at the very outset of Israeli history, and the contours of the relationship are complex, confusing, and sometimes contradictory. But the fact of the difficult relationship helps explain the occasional feelings of alienation by one side or the other.

Despite the friction among the crew members, the *Tradewinds* made it across the Atlantic Ocean and stopped in the Azores before reaching Lisbon.

There "Captain Diamond," the local Haganah representative, waited for them. Yehoshua Baharav, bearing a Canadian passport and the appropriate false identity papers, was an adventurer who came from a kibbutz and had already helped other Aliyah Bet ships.

True to their roughhouse reputation, some of the American members of the crew went to a local bar and got into a fight with some British men. Captain Diamond paid for all the damages they had inflicted, but the police didn't accept his story and, just as the *Tradewinds* prepared to leave Lisbon, the chief of the secret police, accompanied by some of his men, boarded the ship. Captain Diamond offered them Brazilian cigars, but they weren't interested. They thought they could get more than cigars because they were looking for terrorists or Communists, and this shipboard crew certainly looked suspicious. The head of the secret police wanted Diamond to come onshore for further investigation. Acting quickly, Diamond spoke in Hebrew, telling the crew to sail without him as a pilot and send the rest of the Portuguese back to shore in another, smaller boat.

The chief of the secret police was furious as he observed the departure of the ship. He grabbed Captain Diamond and tore his jacket. Other police officers surrounded the captain and started hitting him. Keeping to his cover story of being a ship's captain for the United Fruit Company, Diamond casually suggested that his company intended to send a number of other ships to Lisbon. Before that could happen, he said, he needed to return to Paris, so he needed his passport and papers back. Diamond was let go, and the tense relationship he developed with the secret police captain paid off later. Two Aliyah Bet ships were berthed in Lisbon and unable to get fuel from a British company. Diamond phoned the captain of the secret police, arranged to pay him a bribe, and the captain made sure the two ships got their fuel.

Once the *Tradewinds* reached Port de Bouc, near Marseilles, the Gentile captain left, although he promised that the next time he would sail all the way home.

While docked in Port de Bouc, the *Tradewinds* acquired another passenger. The Reverend John Stanley Grauel was a Methodist minister. He would later play a crucial part in the United Nations' decision to partition Palestine (see chapter 2).

Grauel had been born in Worcester, Massachusetts, and after his theological training, learned about the Holocaust from his friend Judge

Joseph Goldberg. Seeking to help the Jews, Grauel joined the Zionist America Palestine Committee (APC). A year later, in 1943, Grauel resigned from his job as a minister and directed the APC's office in Philadelphia. It was through this job that Grauel met David Ben-Gurion and learned of the Haganah's Aliyah Bet activities. Grauel immediately saw such an effort as crucial and so, continuing to work for the America Palestine Committee, this Methodist minister became a Haganah agent.

He had been on board the S.S. *Exodus* (discussed below) but had left the ship in order to obtain a British visa so that he could legally enter Palestine. He would serve as a correspondent for the *Churchman*, an Episcopalian journal, and in that journalistic role, Grauel was assigned the task of telling the *Exodus*'s story to the world.

The *Exodus* had sailed without him, so he boarded the *Tradewinds*, which would drop him in Italy so that he could again board the *Exodus*. Grauel was not happy aboard the *Tradewinds*, not used to its harsh conditions. He once stood at the ship's guardrail and announced that "when this is over, I'm going to write a book about it and call it the Via Dolorosa," referring to the street in the Old City of Jerusalem that supposedly was the path Jesus walked on his way to the crucifixion. The street's name literally means the "Way of Sorrows" or the "Way of Suffering."

In Provender on the coast in northwest Italy, the *Tradewinds* sat next to the *Exodus*. Ada Sereni, who headed the Italian branch of Aliyah Bet, visited the *Tradewinds*. Sereni's more famous husband, Enzo, had been sent to parachute over Europe in 1944, was captured, and was murdered in Dachau. Ada Sereni had difficult organizational tasks. She had to find the various refugees a place to live and then organize their journeys to the Land of Israel. Over the course of several years, she aided twenty-eight thousand Jewish refugees in their quest to make aliyah. In all, thirty-eight ships sailed to Palestine from Italy.

Sereni oversaw the boarding of passengers onto the *Tradewinds* in two separate locations. There were fourteen hundred refugees aboard. The ship began its voyage to Palestine, encountering the all-too-normal problem of seasickness, which the crew tried to control with tea and vitamins. The illness wasn't helped by the standard operating procedure of having the passengers stay below decks and take turns going onto the deck for fresh air.

More than a week after the voyage began, a British airplane buzzed the *Tradewinds* twice. The crew made a desperate effort to change the ship's appearance by taking apart some of the its structural features. This effort did not succeed; British warships soon came into view. The passengers were told to go on deck and prepare to resist the British.

It was at this time that the ship openly declared itself as a Zionist vessel by changing its name to the *Hatikvah* (Hebrew for hope and eventually the name of the Israeli national anthem).

One of the British destroyers sailed beside the *Hatikvah*. Someone on the destroyer yelled out the standard statement: "Your voyage is illegal. Your ship is unseaworthy. In the name of humanity, surrender." A British officer on the destroyer yelled out, asking the captain of the ship to identify himself. The *Hatikvah* officers instead put forward a ten-year-old boy, put a cap on his head, and taught him enough English to yell back, "I am the captain."

After a failed attempt to board the *Hatikvah*, several British marines, fully prepared for battle, fought resistors and climbed aboard. Concerned about children and pregnant women, those involved in the resistance limited their actions but remained spirited. The British then fired tear gas into the engine room, forcing the men inside to come out and giving the British access to the newly improvised steering mechanism.

On May 17, 1947, the *Hatikvah* was towed into the port in Haifa. There were twenty-seven Americans in the crew, and they mostly went with the refugees to Cyprus. However, six were arrested. One of the Americans swam ashore and claimed to be a student at the Technion Institute. Naturally, the school officials immediately supported his claim.

Those Americans who were sent to Cyprus stayed there for fourteen weeks. One of the Americans met a woman he would later marry. Three of the Americans worked with the Haganah in an attempt to build an escape tunnel from the camp. One hundred and fifty feet away from the camp stood a clump of trees, and that was the planned destination for the tunnel. The men dug down ten feet and then began to dig toward the trees. The Americans worked on the tunnel for two weeks, but then were needed for other work. The Haganah eventually finished the tunnel and used it for successful escapes.

The new task for the Americans in the detention camp was a delicate one. They were ordered to build a bomb in order to sink a British prison ship. After the bomb was built, it would, in theory at least, be smuggled onto the ship and then detonated.

The Haganah sent detonators and gelignite along with other necessary materials to Cyprus. The Americans cut the camp's barbed wire and retrieved all these bomb-making supplies. The Americans succeeded in their task, but unfortunately the British had spotted them and announced harsh consequences if those who escaped didn't turn themselves in to the authorities. The Haganah members wrote a note using false names and, enclosing local currency, said they simply were upset by always being behind the barbed wire and had gone into the town for some enjoyment. This seemed to satisfy the British authorities, and so the Haganah went about their task of assembling a bomb.

The volunteers tried to hide the gelignite inside bars of soap, but this proved unworkable because the change in the bars was easily detected. The bomb builders solved their concealment problems by turning to tubes of shaving cream. The cream was extracted, the gelignite inserted, and a topping of the cream was put in place.

The prison ship *Empire Lifeguard* became the target vessel. It was American sailors from the *Hatikvah* along with the man in charge of the bomb who completed the work. The shaving-tube bomb was assembled. A suspicious British officer opened the tube and squeezed. The shaving cream topping came out, and the tube passed British inspection. It turned out more gelignite was needed. A nurse accompanying an ill patient carried five pounds of the dangerous explosive in her handbag. An American volunteer took the gelignite when the nurse boarded the *Empire Lifeguard*. One British officer sought to examine the bag, but someone else vouched for the nurse. Men strapped rubber sacks onto their backs, hidden by their shirts.

A British prison ship's interior contained very large wire cages. The first American on board the *Empire Lifeguard* suddenly became fearful when he saw the cages. He thought the other men involved in the bomb effort might be sent to different cages. Thinking quickly, he enlisted the aid of various women in the cage. He pointed out the Americans on the team, and the women, each selecting a man, called out to them under the pretense that the men were their husbands. The guards permitted the "husbands" and "wives" to be together. The group of conspirators united again, and the leader from Palestine received a hacksaw from one of the Americans who came on board. The leader then asked everyone to start singing.

The passengers broke into a hearty song while the leader sawed the hatch cover's lock on the floor of the cage. Once he opened the cover, there was a light. He immediately closed the cover and gave a knife to one of the Americans along with the order to kill any sailors the Americans encountered. The Americans descended, but no killing was required because the hatch was empty. They went about assembling the bomb except for the detonator and returned to the cage. They set to sail overnight for their destination in the Land of Israel.

Biding their time, the bomb plotters waited until the prison ship was two hours from the Haifa port. At that point, the kibbutznik in charge placed the detonator in its proper place. The detonator had a timer and therefore would explode without anyone having to trigger the bomb. The plotters were pleased. They had performed the seemingly impossible and smuggled a bomb aboard a prison ship and then armed it to explode.

But plots that often sound elegant and brilliant in the planning stage sometimes have difficulties when the chaotic facts of reality enter. The *Empire Lifeguard* kept moving forward, and then it didn't. The *Lifeguard*'s propeller simply stopped and therefore so did the ship. Now all the refugees were on board with a bomb ready and timed to explode. Stuck inside an iron cage, the prisoners were in a near panic. They spoke to the man who had placed and set the bomb. They told him the anchor had been dropped, which meant the ship was not going anywhere. Perhaps, they strongly suggested, the detonator should be removed.

And it was there that the curse of planning without seeing the consequences of reality entered. The bomb setter said, "They taught me how to put it on. They didn't tell me how to take it off."

The next thought was that the British needed to be told about the bomb. The benefit of that was that maybe, but only maybe, someone was on board who could remove the detonator. The price of informing the British was that the entire effort, the incredible work that had been done to prepare, the massive publicity that was needed, would be lost.

Émile Durkheim, the French sociologist, once distinguished between chronological time, the time that passes according to an objective measuring instrument such as a clock, and psychological time, the subjective feeling of how much time has passed. Psychological time passed excruciatingly slowly. The chronological time was, however, about ten minutes before the anchor was brought up and the ship again sailed toward Haifa and then entered the harbor.

The last of the refugee passengers of the *Empire Lifeguard* had made it to shore when there was an explosion. The refugees didn't look back at the ship. One of the British soldiers suddenly recalled the nurse and her handbag and called out about her. The *Empire Lifeguard* took on too much water, and the ship sank in the harbor. The furious British, however, were never able to capture the bombers. The rousing success of the bombing operation was not without cost. After it took place, the British charged the Jewish Agency a fee for every passenger sent to Cyprus.

The Americans were sent to Athlit, a British camp where a group of American Jewish leaders visited them. One of the leaders was Judith Epstein, who served two terms as president of Hadassah, the prominent Zionist organization for women. Epstein recognized one of the men behind the barbed wire.

"Harold Katz," she asked, "what are you doing behind barbed wire?"

Katz evidently recalled a story about Henry David Thoreau. The transcendental philosopher had once refused to pay a tax for the Mexican war and was jailed. His friend and mentor Ralph Waldo Emerson visited him there and, as Judith Epstein had inquired, asked Thoreau why he was in jail.

Harold Katz responded in the way Thoreau had. "Mrs. Epstein, what are you doing not behind barbed wire?"

The Americans were eventually released.

Without doubt, the *Exodus* was the most famous of the sixty-four ships that took part in Aliyah Bet operations. For better or worse, the story of the *Exodus* is somewhat confusing because of the extraordinary 1957 novel titled *Exodus*, written by Leon Uris. That fictional tale is not historically synonymous with the actual ship named *Exodus*.

The novel took on a life of its own. In the United States, it stirred millions of readers, some of whom had still been uninformed about the Holocaust or unable to speak about it openly. Others had not fully followed the birth of Israel and began to see its founders and citizens as heroic. In the Soviet Union, where the novel was banned, the illegal Russian translation was handed from person to person and had an enormous influence on the growth of Zionism among the Jews under Soviet rule, eventually playing a major role in the effort to allow those Jews their own exodus. The power of the novel multiplied many times when Otto Preminger made the novel into a film starring Paul Newman. In Uris's novel, there was a hunger strike and the *Exodus* had three hundred refugee children. The real *Exodus* had 4,550 passengers on board whom the British deported to Germany. As if the two stories weren't complicated enough, Uris told the story of the true *Exodus* in his fictional tale but gave the ship another name. That story is told in book 1, chapter 27.

The real story of the *Exodus* begins with its original name: the *President Warfield*. The ship, named after Solomon Davies Warfield, the president of the Old Bay Line that originally launched the ship, was given over to the British Ministry of War in 1942.

After the United Kingdom returned the vessel in 1944, it became an American naval ship. It left active service in 1945 and was returned to the War Shipping Administration.

The Haganah became interested in the vessel as a gamble. It believed that the British would fear for the publicity that would come from damage to the ship and harm or death to the passengers since it was in such terrible condition. The idea was that the fearful British would therefore let the ship go past the blockade. Additionally, just as the Haganah became interested in the ship, the British announced that illegal immigrants to Palestine would be sent to Cyprus. The Haganah believed the appropriate response was that capture should be resisted. The *President Warfield* was both fast and built not to overturn. If the British tried to ram the ship, its steel hull would allow it to remain sturdy. Finally, the British destroyers were smaller than the *President Warfield*, thus adding to the difficulty of British marines trying to board it. The ship was too big to hide, so from the outset it would be different. Its objective was not to sneak past the blockade, which, given the ship's size, was virtually impossible. Rather this ship was meant to be an act of open defiance. Plans rarely worked as well as this one did.

Therefore, on November 9, 1946, the Haganah purchased the *President Warfield* from the War Shipping Administration and, in keeping with its pattern of connecting the modern Jewish state with the history of the Jewish people, renamed it the *Exodus 1947*. Of course, this choice was, intentionally or not, brilliant because everyone was familiar with the biblical story of the Exodus, so the ship's name was immediately recognizable and invoked sympathy. After considerable work on the ship, it departed Baltimore on February 25, 1947, and headed toward the Land of Israel. Before its departure, on February 16, 1947, the Zionists from Baltimore boarded the ship for a ceremony. The American volunteers took the Haganah oath. They each got a Bible and a sweater. Danny Shind was there, as was Rudolf G. Sonneborn, whose institute provided so much support to Haganah efforts. So was I. F. Stone, the reporter. Also, during the week prior to departure, one of the American Jewish volunteers married a Catholic woman in a shipboard ceremony on the *Exodus*. Maryland law required someone from the clergy to perform the ceremony, and so the Methodist minister John Stanley Grauel officiated.

The ship stopped at a port near Marseilles to let refugees board. As the boarding continued, a Royal Air Force plane circled overhead. A British warship was there shortly after the *Exodus 1947* began its voyage in the overnight hours of July 11. It flew a flag from Honduras. The ship had 1,600 men, 1,282 women, and 1,612 children and teenagers. Ike Aronowicz, age twenty-three, was the captain, and Yossi Harel, a sixth-generation Jerusalemite and longtime fighter and intelligence agent from the Haganah, served as the ship's commander.

British destroyers and planes began to track the *Exodus* as soon as it left the harbor. One of the destroyers tried to contact the ship, but the *Exodus* did not respond.

The refugees on board, knowing that eventually the British would attempt to stop or capture the ship, developed a rigorous organization. A food detail was established. It took dried rations and heavy buckets filled with barley soup to the passengers. Each person on board got a liter of drinking water each day.

Members of Zionist youth groups served as guides to movement aboard the ship. Passengers, except for children and pregnant women, were assigned specific jobs. The *Exodus* had turned into a small community, almost a kibbutz at sea.

The refugees were intensely curious about how the world perceived them, so the public address system had news broadcasts in Yiddish, Hungarian, English, and Hebrew. To make the voyage more pleasant, the chorale from Beethoven's Ninth Symphony was played as well. A handwritten newspaper was produced on board to keep the passengers informed. Many of the passengers, knowing they would need to speak Hebrew when they reached the Land of Israel, asked for Hebrew lessons, which were given. The crew tried to entertain the passengers, and the passengers in turn engaged in their own entertainment by singing. Unfortunately, there was constant seasickness. One woman died giving birth to a son. The *Exodus* stopped at sunset for the funeral, with the crew becoming an honor guard. Sadly, the baby died several weeks later in Haifa.

As the ship neared land, the passengers divided into different sections and began to prepare for what they expected to be the coming resistance.

On the day of the funeral, the Haganah gave new orders to the ship. They were to dash for the beach on July 17 by staying outside the territorial waters of Palestine until the last possible second and then head directly for the beach. The Haganah's plan was to have thousands of people on the beach ready to meet them.

A confrontation was getting close. The British now had assembled a small armada. Their escort ship was there and was joined by the *Ajax*, a cruiser, four destroyers, a frigate, and two minesweepers. The Americans joined with others on board the ship to send a mock salute to the British as the public address system blasted out Elgar's *Pomp and Circumstance*.

The crew began to make final preparations for an attack by the British. Crew members put wire mesh all around the promenade deck and across any openings. Pipes were set up to bring oil at the moment the British boarded in order to make the invaders slip. Sandbags were put around the wheelhouse to keep the British from gaining access to the steering mechanism.

It was two in the morning on Friday, July 18. The ship was still twenty-three miles from Haifa's coast. At 3:30 a.m., they were to change course, go north, and head for the proposed landing area.

The British attacked before the crew could begin to change course. First, the British vessels turned on their searchlights. It was that night that the ship we know as the *Exodus* acquired that name. The *President Warfield* had officially changed its name to *Exodus 1947*, and in case the British needed a reminder, the crew hung blue-and-white Jewish flags with the English-language sign "Haganah Ship—Exodus 1947."

The British declared that the *Exodus* had entered Palestine's territorial waters and ordered the ship to halt in order to be towed to Haifa.

The *Exodus*, of course, had no intention of surrendering to the British. The ship turned in a virtually hopeless attempt to flee. In response, destroyers on both sides of the *Exodus* attacked and rammed the ship. The pipes that had been so carefully set up to spill oil suddenly snapped.

The British set up their landing bridges to reach the deck of the *Exodus*. British marines and sailors, dressed for battle, charged across. It didn't take long for the British marines to take the wheelhouse. As they did, the British clubbed one American, Bill Bernstein, until he was unconscious. Another American was shot in the jaw. One American volunteer and a Haganah agent acted quickly and disconnected the steering mechanism from its place in the wheelhouse. The ship then began an erratic course, going deliberately into any British ship that came near it. The British destroyers, one after another, became damaged from these encounters. The British had gotten only forty men on board the *Exodus*, but as daybreak neared, they began to fire using small arms. Two Jewish passengers were killed, including a fifteen-year-old orphan who was mortally wounded with a shot to the head.

The battle lasted until 5:15 a.m. At that point, the *Exodus*'s leaders, realizing that there was no hope that they could land their ship safely, agreed to surrender. Bill Bernstein, the American who had been knocked out in the struggle over the wheelhouse, was in the captain's cabin. Bernstein was dying. Other members of the crew surrounded him but painfully realized they had no way to save him. In all, 146 Jews on the *Exodus* had received an injury. Twenty-eight of them were sent to a hospital.

An American volunteered to take over the captain's role so that the crew members who were volunteers from America and the Land of Israel could either hide or pretend to be one of the passengers. At four in the afternoon, just as the passengers were preparing for the impending Sabbath, the *Exodus* was towed into Haifa. Three Americans who had served as crew members were arrested. They received a temporary release from jail three days later so they could serve as pallbearers at Bill Bernstein's funeral. The three were later deported. A work crew, all

Jewish, came on board to clean the ship. The Haganah members who had remained hidden on board simply walked off with this cleaning crew.

By that time, the story of the *Exodus 1947* had made its way around the world. Sensitive to public opinion, the British concluded that the simplest approach was to avoid sending the passengers to Cyprus but rather send them back to France, from where they had sailed. Ernest Bevin, Britain's foreign secretary, was not being kind. He was being characteristically cunning. He wanted to send a loud message to any country that had thought about helping future refugees. The British would capture those refugees and send them right back to where they had sailed from. Those countries would be "stuck" with them.

Once the *Exodus* had been brought to Haifa's port, the passengers were transferred to three other ships, which would be used to deport them. Tellingly, the entire transfer of passengers was witnessed by members of the U.N. Special Committee on Palestine (UNSCOP), which the United Nations had established on May 15, 1947, after the British asked that a special committee be established to report to the General Assembly. (More on the United Nations' role in partitioning the land can be found in chapter 2.) The UNSCOP witnesses could see for themselves the determination of the Jews and the situation of the British.

On July 28, the three British ships reached Port de Bouc, near Marseilles, and dropped their anchors outside French territorial waters. The French announced that the passengers could disembark and enter the country only if they voluntarily agreed to do so. Of course, Haganah agents were grateful for this opportunity because it offered them another chance to resist the British. Sixty of the passengers, all ill or elderly, stated that they wished to go ashore.

The ships remained offshore for more than three weeks. With the French refusing to allow the ships to land, the British were forced to switch strategies. On August 21, the British Foreign Office had formulated its plan. If the Jewish refugees refused to go ashore voluntarily, they would be deported at 6 p.m. the following day to the British zone in occupied Germany. The destination, of course, was filled with emotional resonance after the Holocaust. The British understood that the public would condemn them for the German plan, but, they concluded, their zone in Germany was the only place they controlled where they could house so many people. So sensitive were the British that on August 22, the Foreign Office sent a cable warning British diplomats that they had to be prepared for an outcry and must deny, in the strongest possible terms, that the Jewish refugees would be sent to former concentration camps or that German guards would be used to maintain control among the Jewish refugees. Indeed, the cable continued, the diplomats were to stress that even British guards would be removed after the passengers had been screened to find Haganah members.

The stubborn British could not see the public relations catastrophe waiting to happen. The passengers continued to refuse debarkation, and so twenty minutes after the deadline had been reached, the prison ships turned and set sail for Germany.

The dispirited passengers, grasping that they were not being sent to Cyprus, began a twenty-four-hour hunger strike and refused to follow British orders in any way. With the whole world watching, the British felt they could not look weak, so they refused to change their plans.

The members of UNSCOP noted this struggle. The ships arrived in Hamburg on September 8. Some passengers on one of the ships staged a sit-down strike. They were dragged ashore. A bomb was found on another vessel. On the third ship, Jews on board refused to disembark and engaged in a two-hour battle. The passengers were met by twenty-five hundred British troops armed with clubs and tear gas.

The refugees were sent to displaced persons camps in Am Stau and Poppendorf. Remarkably, one American volunteer had become romantically involved with a refugee and accompanied her. When they reached their internment camp, they found her mother. The refugee had assumed that her mother had been murdered by the Nazis.

The story of *Exodus 1947* was a public relations disaster for the British and a great success for the Zionist cause. An outcry was heard around the world, stirred in part by the vivid journalistic descriptions of the living conditions of the refugees who had been returned to Germany. Members of the U.S. Congress were loud and clear in denouncing British actions. President Harry S. Truman expressed keen displeasure in a characteristically clear voice. On July 25, a memorial for Bill Bernstein was held at Madison Square Park in New York. Twenty thousand people attended. In Britain itself, the opposition Conservative Party was headed by Winston Churchill, the former prime minister and the man who had warned the people of the Nazi peril and aroused British sentiment against Hitler, it sometimes seemed singlehandedly, and who had so masterfully run the war effort. The Tories bitterly attacked the Labour government for its incredibly inept handling of the entire *Exodus 1947* incident. The Jews in the Land of Israel, sensing that their moment in history was upon them, began increasing acts of rebellion against British rule. It was at this time that the UNSCOP recommended partition.

The existence of the refugees in detention centers was compared to their lives in concentration camps. The perception was compounded by the British again being tone-deaf. The British had a military practice of employing local civilians for jobs that did not require security clearance. That protocol may have made sense in ordinary circumstances, but in this case it turned out that Germans were among those who worked inside the camp where the Jewish refugees were held. The Zionists kept accusing the British of being cruel and being insensitive about how they treated survivors of the Nazis. With the blazing heat of a world spotlight on them, the increasingly uneasy British were anxious. By October 1947, the Foreign Office sent a telegram to the German camps, wanting confirmation that barbed wire was not being used to surround the camp and that Germans were not guarding the Jews.

The Jewish leaders in the camps wrote a telegram on October 20, 1947, to express their hopes and expectations: "Nothing will deter us from Palestine. Which jail we go to is up to you [the British]. We did not ask you to reduce our rations; we did not ask you to put us in Poppendorf and Am Stau."

And then the conditions got worse. The refugees had been housed in Nissen huts and tents at Am Stau and Poppendorf, but the weather, rainy and cold, made the tents unsuitable.

Once in another setting, many of the refugees were smuggled into the American zone, where they attempted, often with success, to make their way to the Land of Israel. Indeed, by April 1948, only eighteen hundred refugees from the original *Exodus 1947* remained in the camps. Those who had attempted to get to Palestine were mostly captured and sent to detention camps on Cyprus. Once the British recognized the State of Israel in January 1949, more than half a year since the state had been declared by David Ben-Gurion and recognized by President Truman acting in the name of the United States, those refugees still held on Cyprus were sent to the new Jewish state, no doubt with hostility and reluctance.

That might have been the end of the affair, except that the Irgun and the followers of Avraham Stern felt they had to get even with the British. There was also a political element to their decision to attack the British. If independence was eventually to take place, the British public would have to be sick of hearing about Palestine, uneasy about how Holocaust survivors were being treated, and angry about how British soldiers had to deal with the upstart Zionists. The British public would have to pressure the government to surrender their mandate, and further, this pressure had to be felt continually until independence finally arrived.

Therefore, on September 29, 1947, the Jews outside the Haganah used a barrel bomb to blow up the ten-story Central Police Headquarters in Haifa. Ten people were killed and fifty-four injured. Thirty-three of the injured were British. A sixteen-year-old, an Arab woman, four Arab police officers, and four British police officers were killed.

The *Exodus 1947* itself suffered the fate of many of the ships that had participated in Aliyah Bet efforts. Because the ships were characteristically unseaworthy, they were moored in the port in Haifa's harbor. History moved relentlessly forward at a rocket's speed for what would become Israel, and the preparations for war and the building of the state left little time for historical reflection or celebrating the ships that that brought freedom to so many. The *Exodus 1947*, damaged, old, incapable of additional military or other use, simply sat there.

Abba Koushi, the mayor of Haifa, proposed in 1951 that an Aliyah Bet museum be built and that the *Exodus 1947*, by then known as the "Ship That Launched a Nation," should be housed there, restored to its sailing condition, and serve as a floating memorial to all that had taken place on its historic voyage. Preparations began to restore the ship, but unfortunately on August 26, 1952, the *Exodus 1947* burned down. The remaining hull was towed and sunk near Shemen Beach in the Kishon River. A dozen years after the fire, a firm from Italy cut the hull into two sections to salvage what remained for scrap metal. The ship sank again. In 1974, there was still another effort to raise what remained of the ship for salvage. The *Exodus* was refloated, but it sank once more. Parts of the ship's hull remained visible. People who wished to fish sometimes went there. Then the Port of Haifa built container ship quay extensions over the remaining parts of the *Exodus*. The quay is currently in a security zone and is not accessible to the public.

There are historical plaques or markers to commemorate the *Exodus 1947* in the United States, France, Italy, and Germany. Ironically, there are no comparable plaques, markers, or memorials in Israel.

The plaque in the United States can be found at the Smithsonian Institution in Washington, DC, along with a model of the *Exodus*. The plaque reads: "Built for the Old Bay Line as the President Warfield, this old steamer later was involved in the Jewish immigration strife on the Palestine coast." It is difficult to imagine a more understated tribute to the heroes who sailed on the *Exodus*. Evidently, there was some dismay with the plaque, so the Smithsonian offered a second plaque. This one was more forthcoming:

> In early 1947, the President Warfield joined the "illegal immigration fleet" transporting refugees from Europe to Palestine, and was renamed Exodus.

On her final voyage in July 1947 with 4550 refugees aboard, Exodus was stopped by British naval units. In the ensuing struggle her American Chief Mate William Bernstein was killed.

Exodus was one of ten vessels in the "illegal immigration fleet" manned by volunteers from the United States, Canada, and Latin America. The fleet pursued its mission against a British blockade of the Palestine Coast during 1946–1948.

The ten vessels are then named and the explanation offered that the plaque was given to the Smithsonian "by the American volunteers in tribute to the spirit of their mission and the courage of their passengers."

Forty years after the voyage of the *Exodus 1947*, in 1987, American veterans of the rescue effort carried a replica of the plaque to Israel, where it was presented to the Clandestine Immigration and Naval Museum in Haifa.

The story of the *Exodus* became a symbol of Holocaust survivors desperately in search of refuge. The story of the refugees on the ship touched the hearts of, among many others, members of the British and American publics. As such, the heroism of the *Exodus* crew and passengers stood as representative of all the incredible crew members, all the brave and sometimes desperate passengers. The story of the *Exodus* was politically potent precisely because it illustrated such desperation and such heroism and cast the British as the villains. The *Exodus* became the most potent political weapon against the British.

CONCLUSION

The Lessons for America and Israel

For many centuries, Jews had both the luxury and horror of not having a political identity in the world. The horrors are all too well known, from the Crusades and ghettos to the polite anti-Semitism and overt discrimination all the way to the devastation of six million murders by the Nazis. The luxury of the Diaspora is more subtle. Without the obligations to defend a homeland, Jews did not have to face the inherent ethical dilemmas of conflict. Jews could, and did, focus on learning and ethics, on being good. Their ethics covered their relations with God, themselves, and others. They couldn't pick up weapons, so they didn't have to consider the moral consequences of doing so. The rise of Zionism changed much in Jewish history, and one of the changes involved how Jews thought about ethics. To this day, some Jews cannot yet reconcile what they think of as Jewish, that is ethical behavior, kindness toward others, and so on, with the terrible obligations of protecting their nation. As Golda Meir so poignantly put it, "When peace comes we may be able to forgive the Arabs for killing our children, but we will not be able to forgive them for forcing us to kill their children."

Such an ethical situation is in many ways at the heart of this book. Some people see the efforts, some extralegal, of Americans, Jews and non-Jews, who helped give birth to Israel as immoral. It is important to make clear moral distinctions. The Jews sought only to provide defense for themselves. The Holocaust didn't cause the birth of Israel, but even at its inception as a modern nation, Israel's founders considered the need for a Jewish state to be vital precisely because of the murderous intentions of those who hated Jews. The Holocaust made such a Zionist assertion horrifyingly clear. Realizing their need for self-protection, drawn to their ancient homeland, the Zionists, from their beginning, sought a way of cooperating with Arabs living in the land.

The actions in this book were sometimes undertaken in desperation, but they were not undertaken in revenge or anger or with a refusal to cooperate with the Arabs living in the land.

It was precisely the historical reality of the moment, the desperate condition of world Jewry, the unique opportunity to revive their state, and the unbelievable coincidence of interests of the United States and the Soviet Union that, among other factors, allowed for the birth of Israel.

The Americans whose stories have been told in this book are genuine heroes. Their activities were the ethical activities of what real politics called for.

The Zionist enterprise, the most significant positive development in modern Jewish history, does not solve every problem. Had there been an Arab acceptance of dividing the land, perhaps history would have unfolded differently. But that was not to be.

We are in an age when the glow of Israel's heroic birth has been dimmed for some. In Europe, there is a resurgence of anti-Semitism. The Palestinian Arabs continue to avoid recognizing a Jewish state in Israel. The Israelis, who acquired land west of the Jordan River in a defensive action undertaken after the Arab nations had taken actions tantamount to a declaration of war, are sometimes accused of the mistreatment of Arabs and being reluctant to enter into a treaty to ensure the creation of a Palestinian Arab state. But the Israelis, weary of wars and terrorism, wary of believing that any peace treaty can be enforced, remain understandably hesitant about giving up any more land after

CONCLUSION

seeing their returned land in the Gaza Strip become the launch pad for Hamas missiles and underground tunnels used to foment terror.

It is just at this moment when Israel is under the microscope that it may be helpful to take a step back, to remember why Israel was needed in the first place and what enormous sacrifices had to be made.

Sometimes it doesn't produce worthwhile results to look backward. In Israel's case, it does, for several reasons. First, the story itself is inspiring. Second, however tangled and complex the Zionist effort has been, it was, given the circumstances, profoundly needed by a deeply wounded Jewish people.

But Israel is not just a country and not just a haven for the Jewish people. It is, as David Ben-Gurion intended, a symbol of hope. Israel's founding father and first prime minister meant for Israel to have a special meaning and follow the Jewish people's historic mission to be a light unto the nations. Ben-Gurion wanted an army that had to fight to be the most moral army that ever was, to be conscious of and careful to avoid civilian casualties. Ben-Gurion wanted the biblical truths that were so hard earned throughout Jewish history to be available to all the peoples of the world. He wanted Jerusalem to radiate as a spiritual center not just for Jews but for people of all faiths. Secular himself, Ben-Gurion saw in Judaism the possibility of human cooperation. He wanted Israel not just to be a nation but to be a guiding light for humanity. In that spirit, Israel's heroic birth should be celebrated.

Israel is a special story in the ongoing narrative of humanity.

These tales of Israel's birth are meant to be inspiring not only for Jews or those who support Israel but for all people who see in this story the story of the human condition, the story of refusing to give up just when all seems lost but instead giving birth to new hope even as such hope is attacked by others.

This is a story of Americans who helped in the birth of Israel—that is, a story that is really about humans who helped in the birth of a new and better tomorrow.

CHRONOLOGY

1945

End of June. David Ben-Gurion arrives in the United States.

July 1. Ben-Gurion holds a meeting at Rudolf Sonneborn's apartment, and the Sonneborn Institute is formed.

August 28. The first post–World War II Aliyah Bet voyage takes place. Thirty-five immigrants aboard the *Dalin* reach the Land of Israel.

September 5. The British restrict Jewish immigration to Palestine to fifteen hundred people every month.

September. Phil Alper hitchhikes to New York.

October. Haim Slavin arrives in the United States to arrange for the purchase of machinery.

1946

January. Jacob Dostrovsky (Yaakov Dori) becomes head of the Haganah delegation in the United States until June 1947.

April. The *Wedgwood* and the *Haganah*, the first two Aliyah Bet boats with American crews, sail from New York.

June 26. The *Josiah Wedgewood*, carrying 1,259 passengers, is intercepted by the British.

July 7. Ben-Gurion is again in New York and asks the Sonneborn Institute to become active.

September 5. The pro-Zionist play *A Flag Is Born* opens in New York.

Fall. Slavin is ordered to leave the United States.

October 17. The Sonneborn Institute decides to raise $10,000 a week to accumulate $1 million by the end of the year.

1947

February 14. Britain refers the question of what to do with Palestine to the United Nations.

February 24. An agent carrying weapons is stopped by authorities at the Canadian border.

May 13. The United Nations appoints a Special Committee on Palestine to study the situation and make recommendations.

June. Shlomo Rabinovich (Shamir) replaces Dostrovsky until February 1948.

July 18. The ship *Exodus* is captured by the British. During the fight, three Jews aboard are killed.

Summer. The secret school is set up in Manhattan.

August 31. The UN Special Committee on Palestine concludes that partition into Jewish and Arab states is the best option.

November. Al Schwimmer begins his efforts.

November 29. The United Nations votes for partition.

December 6. Beginning of the U.S. arms embargo on sales to countries in the Middle East.

1948

January 3. A courier is stopped after authorities discover TNT at a Jersey City pier.

January 28. Golda Meir's tour in the United States to raise money begins in Chicago.

February. Hank Greenspun goes to Hawaii to get arms.

February. Teddy Kollek replaces Rabinovich until April 1949.

February 21. Eddie Jacobson sends a telegram to President Harry S. Truman, asking him to meet with Chaim Weizmann.

February 27. Truman refuses Jacobson's request.

March 13. Eddie Jacobson arrives unannounced at the White House to speak with his friend Harry Truman.

March 18. Truman meets Chaim Weizmann.

March 19. Ambassador Warren Austin at the United Nations announces that partition is no longer an option.

May 14, late morning Eastern Standard Time (EST). Israel declares itself a free nation as of midnight on May 15, or 6 p.m. EST May 14.

May 14, 6:11 p.m. EST. The United States offers the new State of Israel de facto recognition.

Late May. Teddy Kollek meets William Levitt and asks for funds.

REFERENCES

BOOKS, ARTICLES, AND ARCHIVES

Almog, Doron. *The Commitment: The Impact of American Jews on the Establishment of the State of Israel post-WWII*. Tel Aviv: Contento De Semrik, 2014.
Amiel, Irit. *Scorched: A Collection of Short Stories on Survivors (Library of Holocaust Testimonies)*. Elstree, UK: Vallentine Mitchell, 2006.
Avriel, Ehud. *Open the Gates!* New York: Atheneum, 1975.
Bachi-Kolodny, Ruth. *Teddy Kollek: The Man, His Life and His Jerusalem*. Jerusalem: Gefen, 2008.
Bercuson, David J. *The Secret Army*. New York: Stein & Day, 1984.
Berkman, Ted. *Cast a Giant Shadow*. Garden City, NY: Doubleday, 1962.
Calhoun, Ricky-Dale. "Arming David: The Haganah's Illegal Arms Procurement Network in the United States, 1945–1949." *Journal of Palestine Studies* 36, no. 4 (Summer 2007): 22–32.
Cohen, Rich. *The Fish That Ate the Whale: The Life and Times of America's Banana King*. New York: Picador, 2013.
Collins, Larry, and Dominique Lapierre. *O Jerusalem!* New York: Simon & Schuster, 1972.
Dewey D. Stone Papers. P-529, 1945; 1946; 1947, Box 02, Folder 05. American Jewish Historical Society, Boston, MA.
Edwards, Terry P. "The Secret Life of the Dror: Part I." *Small Arms Defense Journal* 7, no. 2 (2015). www.sadefensejournal.com/wp/?p=3073.
———. "The Secret Life of the Dror: Part II." *Small Arms Defense Journal* 7, no. 3 (2015). www.sadefensejournal.com/wp/?p=3141.
Federal Bureau of Investigation. "Irgun Zvai Leumi." *FBI Records: The Vault*. https://vault.fbi.gov/Irgun%20Zvai%20Leumi.
Federal Bureau of Investigation. "Zionist Organization of America." *FBI Records: The Vault*. https://vault.fbi.gov/Zionist%20Organization%20of%20America.
Feinberg, Abraham. "The Anatomy of a Commitment." *Rehovot*, Spring 1974.
Folsing, Albrecht. *Albert Einstein: A Biography*. New York: Penguin, 1998.
Gerstl, Hugo N. *Against All Odds: The Magnificent Trio That Built the Israeli Air Force*. Monterey, CA: Samuel Wachtman's Sons, 2012.

Gilbert, Martin. *Churchill and the Jews: A Lifelong Friendship.* New York: Holt, 2007.

Glassman, David. "New York, 1947: Buying Arms for Palestine." In *Builders and Dreamers,* edited by J. J. Goldberg and Elliot King. Cornwall, ON: Cornwall Books, 1993.

Grauel, John Stanley, as told to Eleanor Elfenbein. *Grauel: An Autobiography.* Freehold, NJ: Ivory House, 1983.

Greenfield, Murray S., and Joseph M. Hochstein. *The Jews' Secret Fleet: The Untold Story of North American Volunteers Who Smashed the British Blockade of Palestine.* Jerusalem: Gefen, 1987.

Greenspun, Hank, with Alex Pelle. *Where I Stand: The Record of a Reckless Man.* New York: McKay, 1967.

Grose, Peter. *Israel in the Mind of America.* New York: Knopf, 1983.

Gruber, Ruth. *Destination Palestine: The Story of the Haganah Ship* Exodus 1947. New York: Current Books, 1948.

Habas, Bracha. *The Gate Breakers.* Translated by David Segal. New York: Herzl Press/Thomas Yoseloff, 1963.

Hammer, Gottlieb. *Good Faith and Credit.* Cranbury, NJ: Cornwall Books, 1985.

Harry Levine Papers. P-592, 1969, Box 01, Folder 02. American Jewish Historical Society, Boston, MA.

Hecht, Ben. *A Child of the Century.* New York: Simon & Schuster, 1954.

———. *Perfidy.* New York: Messner, 1961.

Heckelman, A. Joseph. *American Volunteers and Israel's War of Independence.* New York: KTAV, 1974.

Holly, David C. *Exodus 1947.* Boston: Little, Brown, 1969.

Ilan, Amitzur. *The Origin of the Arab-Israeli Arms Race: Arms, Embargo, Military Power and Decision in the 1948 Palestine War.* New York: New York University Press, 1996.

"The Jews of America and the Establishment of the State of Israel." Seminar. Ben-Gurion University of the Negev, April 30, 1985.

Judis, John B. *Genesis: Truman, American Jews, and the Origins of the Arab/Israeli Conflict.* New York: Farrar, Straus & Giroux, 2014.

Kaufman, Menahem. *An Ambiguous Partnership: Non-Zionists and Zionists in America, 1939–1948.* Detroit: Wayne State University Press, 1991.

Klinger, Jerry. "Reverend John Stanley Grauel, the Man Who Helped Make Israel Possible." *Jewish Magazine,* June 2008. www.jewishmag.com/134mag/exodus_grauel/exodus_grauel.htm.

Klich, Ignacio. "Latin America, the United States, and the Birth of Israel: The Case of Somoza's Nicaragua." *Journal of Latin American Studies* 20, no. 2 (November 1988): 389–432.

Kollek, Teddy. *For Jerusalem: A Life.* New York: Random House, 1978.

Kurzman, Dan. *Ben-Gurion: Prophet of Fire.* New York: Simon & Schuster, 1983.

———. *Genesis 1948.* New York: World Publishing Company, 1970.

Levin, Marlin. *Balm in Gilead: The Story of Hadassah.* New York: Schocken, 1973.

Medoff, Rafael. "Ben Hecht's 'A Flag Is Born': A Play That Changed History." Washington, DC: David S. Wyman Institute for Holocaust Studies, 2004. www.wymaninstitute.org/articles/2004-04-flagisborn.php.

———. *Militant Zionism in America: The Rise and Impact of the Jabotinsky Movement in the United States, 1926–1948.* Tuscaloosa: University of Alabama Press, 2002.

———. "New Yorkers Who Fought for the Independence of Zion." *Midstream,* May 2008. www.thefreelibrary.com/New+Yorkers+who+fought+for+the+independence+of+Zion.-a0179159193.

REFERENCES

Meir, Golda. *My Life*. New York: Putnam: 1975.
"Operation Oasis: Reception into British Zone of Germany of Jewish Immigrants." National Archives—British Foreign Office. Reference: FO 945/762. 1947.
Orbach, Michael. "The *Hatikvah* Sailed On: Paul Kaye, a Hero of Aliyah Bet, Tells His Story." *Jewish Star*, April 21, 2010. www.thejewishstar.com/stories/The-HaTikva-sailed-on-Paul-Kaye-a-hero-of-Aliyah-Bet-tells-hisstory,1679?page=1&content_source=PAUL KAYE.
Patek, Artur. *Jews on Route to Palestine: 1934–1944*. Krakow: Jagiiellonian University Press, 2013. www.wuj.pl/UserFiles/File/FRAGMENTY/Patek%20fragment(1).pdf.
Penslar, Derek J. *Jews and the Military: A History*. Princeton, NJ: Princeton University Press, 2013.
Postal, Bernard, and Henry W. Levy. *And the Hills Shouted for Joy*. New York: McKay, 1973.
Radosh, Allis, and Ronald Radosh. *A Safe Haven: Harry S. Truman and the Founding of Israel*. New York: Harper, 2009.
Rapoport, Louis. *Shake Heaven and Earth: Peter Bergson and the Struggle to Rescue the Jews of Europe*. Jerusalem: Gefen, 1999.
Rockaway, Robert A. *But He Was Good to His Mother: The Lives and Crimes of Jewish Gangsters*. Jerusalem: Gefen, 2000.
Rose, Norman. *"A Senseless, Squalid War": Voices from Palestine, 1945–1948*. London: Random House, 2010.
Rudolf G. Sonneborn Papers, 1919–1973. American Jewish Archives, Boston, MA.
Sachar, David B. *David K. Niles and United States Policy toward Palestine: A Case Study in American Foreign Policy*. Cambridge, MA: Harvard University, 1959.
Sasson, Theodore. *The New American Zionism*. New York: New York University Press, 2013.
Schlussel, Debbie. "Exclusive: Letter Details Secret American Network That Helped Israel Become a State." Debbie Schlussel website, May 6, 2014. www.debbieschlussel.com/71226/exclusive-letter-details-secret-american-group-that-helped-israel-become-a-state/.
Sharef, Zeev. *Three Days*. London: Allen, 1962.
Silverberg, Robert. *If I Forget Thee, O Jerusalem*. New York: Pyramid Books, 1972.
Slater, Leonard. *The Pledge*. Bloomington, IN: iUniverse, 2000.
Smith, Grant. "Israel's First US Espionage and Smuggling Network." Antiwar.com, May 30, 2014. http://original.antiwar.com/smith-grant/2014/05/29/israels-first-us-espionage-and-smuggling-network/.
Snetsinger, John. *Truman, the Jewish Vote, and the Creation of Israel*. Stanford, CA: Hoover Institution Press, 1974.
Sonneborn, Charles B. *The Time Has Come: The Role of Rudolf Sonneborn as Catalyst for Israel*. Bloomington, IN: Trafford, 2007.
Stone, I. F. *Underground to Palestine*. New York: Boni and Gaer, 1946.
Syrkin, Marie. *Golda Meir: Israel's Leader*. New York: Putnam, 1969.
Uris, Leon. *Exodus*. New York: Doubleday, 1958.
Urofsky, Melvin I. *We Are One! American Jewry and Israel*. Garden City, NY: Anchor Press, 1978.
Weisgal, Meyer W. *So Far: An Autobiography*. London: Weidenfeld & Nicolson, 1971.
Weiss, Jeffrey, and Craig Weiss. *I Am My Brother's Keeper: American Volunteers in Israel's War for Independence, 1947–1949*. Atglen, PA: Schiffer, 2004.
Weizmann, Chaim. *Trial and Error*. New York: Schocken, 1966.

"What Should Be the Attitude and Relationship of American Jewry, and Particularly A.J.C., toward Israel and Its Problems?" American Jewish Archives, Boston, MA, September 22, 1948. http://ajcarchives.org/ajcarchive/DigitalArchive.aspx.

WEBSITES

Abba Hillel Silver website. www.clevelandjewishhistory.net/silver/home.html.
Exodus 1947 website. www.exodus1947.com/.
Letter from Rudolf G. Sonneborn October 5, 1950, American Jewish Joint Distribution Archives. http://search.archives.jdc.org/multimedia/Documents/NY_AR_45-54/NY_AR 45-54_Orgs/NY_AR45-54_00184/NY_AR45-54_00184_0588.pdf.
World Machal: Volunteers from Overseas in the Israel Defense Forces. www.machal.org.il/
"Recognition of Israel," Harry S. Truman Library and Museum. www.trumanlibrary.org/hst/h.htm.
Recognition of the State of Israel Collection, Harry S. Truman Library and Museum. www.trumanlibrary.org/whistlestop/study_collections/israel/large/.
Rudolf Sonneborn—Zionist Mission to Palestine, 1919 (blog). http://rudolfsonneborn.blogspot.com/.
"Aliyah Bet List 2," Aliyah Bet Project, Paul H. Silverstone website. www.paulsilverstone.com/immigration/Primary/Aliyah/shiplist2.php.
Sonneborn Family Collection. http://archive.org/stream/sonnebornfamilyc01sonn/sonneborn familyc01sonn_djvu.txt.

FILMS

Dvir, Boaz. *A Wing and a Prayer*. PBS, 2015.
Goldstein, Scott. *Where I Stand: The Hank Greenspun Story*. SGP Media, 2008.
Levin, Meyer. *The Illegals*. World Zionist Organization, 1948. DVD, Ergo Media, 1996.
———. *The Unafraid*. Meyer Levin, 1977. VHS, Ergo Media, 1987.
"Murray Greenfield, 'Aliyah Bet.'" *L'Chayim*. JBS, 2015. www.youtube.com/watch?v=tsyZmt5sOVU.
Rodgers, Elizabeth, and Robby Henson. *Exodus 1947*. Maryland Public Television, 1997.
Rosenthal, Alan. *Waves of Freedom*. Biblical Productions, 2008.
Spielberg, Nancy, prod. *Above and Beyond*. Directed by Roberta Grossman. Playmount Productions, 2014.

INDEX

Adler, Stella, 117
Alper, Phil, 57–60, 63, 65, 78, 79
Arazi, Yehuda, 76–77
Ash, William C., 134

Balfour Declaration, 25
Begin, Menachem, 32, 39–40
Ben-Gurion, David, 11–24, 40, 46, 51, 53, 56
Bergson, Peter, 115–118
Bernstein, Nahum, 74–75
Bevin, Ernest, 24
Brandeis, Louis, 21
Brando, Marlon, 120–123, 126
Broad, Shepard, 19, 20
Bunche, Ralph, 30–31

Churchill, Winston, 13
Clifford, Clark, 42, 49, 52
Cohen, Mickey, 118–119

Dostrovsky, Jacob, 65, 68–69, 70, 89

Einstein, Albert, 49–50
Ekdahl, Carl, 60–62, 65
Epstein, Eliahu, 52
Exodus (ship), 147, 152–162

Felix, Michael, 92
A Flag Is Born, 120–128
Fliderblum, Dan, 70

Grauel, Reverend John Stanley, 30, 146–147
Greenfield, Murray S., 144
Greenspun, Hank, 106, 111–112

Haganah, 15
Hecht, Ben, 118, 119–128, 129
Herman, Pee-wee, 98
Herzl, Theodor, 3
Holocaust, 27
Hoover, J. Edgar, 67
Hotel Fourteen, 69

Irgun, 115

Jabotinsky, Vladimir, 115
Jacobson, Eddie, 43–45, 53

Kaye, Paul, 1–2
Kollek, Teddy, 5, 82–84

Lenart, Lou, 96
Levitt, William, 5, 83
Luciano, Charles "Lucky," 95

Magnes, Judah, 49–50
Marcus, David "Mickey," 98–100
Marshall, George C., 42, 51
Marx Brothers, 117
Medoff, Rafael, 117, 124–125, 126–127
Meir, Golda, 4, 39–53, 80–82, 163

Muni, Paul, 122, 138

Nathan, Robert, 67
Niles, David K., 29, 31, 35, 36, 42, 52

Palestine, 7–9, 25
Peel Commission, 26–27

Rabinovich, Shlomo, 73–74, 90–91
Ross, Barney, 119
Rubenfeld, Milton, 97–98

Schalit, Elie, 64–65, 68
Schindler, Irvin "Swifty," 93–94
Schulman, Paul, 137
Schwimmer, Al, 89–92, 93, 100–101, 106, 111, 112
Shiloah, Reuven, 14
Shind, Danny, 89, 133, 134

Silver, Abba Hillel, 21–23, 39, 42–43
Sinatra, Frank, 117
Slavin, Haim, 55–57, 58–60, 61–63, 65
Sonneborn, Rudolf, 15–24, 71–73, 85
Stone, I. F., 135–136, 141–142

Truman, Harry, 27, 29, 41, 42, 44–45, 46, 47, 48, 52

United Nations, 34, 37
Uris, Leon, 152

Weisgal, Meyer, 15, 17
Weizmann, Chaim, 13, 45, 48, 50–51, 52
Westheimer, Dr. Ruth, 97
Wise, Stephen, 21

Zemurray, Samuel, 137

South Huntington   JUL 05 2017